THE
DIVINE PLOTLINE

How God Uses Trials, Triumphs, and Transformation to Write Your Story

CHELSEA FAIN
with contribution chapter from
Pastor Jennifer Neuschwander

Harrisburg, Oregon

Scripture quotations are from the ESV® Bible (The Holy Bible, English Standard Version®), copyright © 2001 by Crossway, a publishing ministry of Good News Publishers. Used by permission. All rights reserved.

The information in this book is intended for informational purposes only. The author is not liable for any outcomes based on the application of this content.

Cover design by Chelsea Fain.
Interior design by Matt Shoemaker.

THE DIVINE PLOTLINE
© 2025 Chelsea Fain
Harrisburg, Oregon 97327
chelseafain.com

ISBN 979-8-90046-862-4

All rights reserved. No part of this publication may be reproduced, stored, or transmitted in any form or by any means, electronic, mechanical, photocopying, recording, or otherwise, without prior written permission of the author/publisher, except in the case of brief quotations used in reviews or critical articles.

For Joshua, my steadfast partner through every plot twist.

For our children, whose stories are still being written by His grace.

"We know that for those who love God all things work together for good, for those who are called according to His purpose."

— Romans 8:28

"Count it all joy, my brothers, when you meet trials of various kinds, for you know that the testing of your faith produces steadfastness. And let steadfastness have its full effect, that you may be perfect and complete, lacking in nothing."

— James 1:2-4

Acknowledgments

To my husband, Joshua: your steady faith and support have been an anchor in many storms and the joy of every triumph. To my four incredible children: thank you for reminding me that God's grace is best seen through childlike trust. To my parents: thank you for your unwavering support and prayers as this book came to life.

To my friends and early readers: thank you for believing in this message and helping me refine it until it shone.

Special thanks to my Launch Team members: Gennie Lynne, Stephanie Richmond, Holly Strasheim, Shelley Ficano, Michelle McElrath, Teresa Zoller, Renee Douffet, Tammy Ballard, Esther Crawford, Dana McGowan, and Bobbi Raffin.

Special thanks to my Beta Readers: Charles Cline, Stacy Soverns, Emily Mann, Melody Miller, Anna Colvin, and Erikka Eveland.

To my intercessor team: thank you for every minute you dedicate to my relationship with God, my ministry, and this book. To my Life Bible Church family: thank you for the way you worship with me and encourage me through every season. Thank you for your support and prayers.

And to every reader walking through a valley: thank you for trusting me with your time and your heart.

Preface

In every great story, there is a turning point. This is often called the "climax," when everything starts to change. For each of us, we live a story, filled with twists and turns. Regardless of where you're at in your journey, there is hope that the Author will turn things around and make your story beautiful. For me, that moment came when I realized God wasn't writing a tragedy; He was weaving a testimony. My testimony.

The Divine Plotline was birthed from my own seasons of suffering and refining. I have learned tremendously over the last several years about the power of the hardest seasons in my life. In those times of heartache, I didn't understand God's plan. In fact, at times, I hated the story I was in. However, looking back now, I can identify His fingerprints all over my pain. And moving forward, I have been able to face new hardships and challenges with a renewed perspective.

My prayer is that as you read, you'll begin to release your past pain and suffering into the hand of the Almighty Potter— fully surrendered to His will and His pruning for your life. As life continues and new trials come your way, I pray you will begin to recognize those seasons as sacred turning points in His greater story.

With love,

Chelsea

Table of Contents

Part 1: Introduction
1. Everyone Loves a Good Story 15
2. What Makes a Good Story? 23
3. Great Value at a Great Cost,
   Chapter by Jennifer Neuschwander 31

Part 2: What Does This Look Like in the Lives of People in the Bible?
4. Job: Trusting the Author in the Darkest Chapter 41
5. Abraham: Walking by Faith When the Map is Blank 51
6. Joseph: From Dreams to Detours 59
7. Moses: When the Wilderness Becomes Holy Ground 67
8. Joshua: The Courage to Conquer 77
9. David: The Crown Forged in the Cave 85
10. The Apostle Paul: When Misplaced Zeal
    Meets Transforming Grace 97

Part 3: Typical Responses to the Stories God Has Placed Us In
11. The Pity-Party Response 113
12. The "THAT'S-NOT-FAIR" Response 117
13. The Angry-at-God Response 121
14. The "Woe-Is-Me-God's-Punishing-Me" Response 127
15. The Apathetic Response 131
16. The Hard-Things-Only-Come-from-Satan Response 137
    Part 3 Reflection: *When God's Path Gets Hard*

Part 4: Next Steps on the Journey
17. Jesus: The Author and Finisher 149
18. Growing in Our Responses to the Potter's Hands 161
19. Closing Thoughts 177
    Afterword 185
    Appendices 187
    References 223

PART I

Introduction

Dear Reader, PLEASE don't brush over this introduction, but spend the extra five minutes reading this brief letter from our hearts. This book is written specifically with the broken, tired, rundown heart in mind. So, whatever your reason, thank you for taking the time to read this. It is an honor to share these pages with you.

I (Chelsea) and my beloved Pastor and friend, Jennifer, have both endured hardships at different points in our lives. We have learned through the midst of those trials the power of God's hand in the hardship and the beauty of God's plan in the story. As Pastor Jenni has been mentoring me over the last several years, she has taught me a lot about how God plans circumstances differently than many people were raised to believe. I had definitely fallen for the Christianese lies that make God sound like a cosmic slot machine of goodness when you're behaving well. Now, I've been learning that the God of the Bible, the God of Creation, actually looks a lot more like a divine author who is willing to let his prized creation (people) walk through challenging circumstances to mature us, bring us closer to Him, and to bring us more in line with His will for our lives.

Here's a hard truth: "Good things" doesn't mean "blessed." Actually, trials and hardships are also a blessing from the Lord! That's one of the driving points of this book that I hope to present to you. God is good in the easy times, *and* he is tender, faithful, gentle, patient, kind, loving, and just in the hard times too.

Maybe you're in one of those seasons of your life where you feel like the walls are caving in around you, your world is crumbling, your heart is breaking, your family is collapsing, your health is failing, and there is absolutely no hope in your situation. You've been screaming at God, "WHERE ARE YOU IN THIS?!" or thinking, "What's the point in even trying anymore?" Whatever your thoughts are right now, this is what I am here to discuss and offer you some hope. I can't promise you a whole world of solutions or personal therapy, but I can promise you a whole lot of Scripture, fresh revelation from the Lord, personal stories of our own sufferings, and God's hand in all the hardships.

All of it starts with a simple concept: stories. Stories have captured the hearts of people throughout time! But why!? And how does that tie into the pain and struggles you might be dealing with right now? Please join us for the following pages as I explain and provide solid evidence of how God, the Master Story Writer, uses a specific storyline structure to mold and craft His children into the men and women He destined them to become. Before we get too tangled in the weeds, though, sit back, kick your feet up, grab your favorite blanket and hot (or iced) beverage, and let's start with the basics: What makes a *good* story?

CHAPTER 1

Everyone Loves a Good Story

Heroes and villains. Damsels in distress. Heroic knights. Daring adventures. Dangerous trials. Wise mentors. Faithful friends. These are the things that make up the most beloved stories. From every culture and every time period, stories have captured the hearts of humanity. Long before written language existed, storytelling thrived — rich, vibrant, and woven into the fabric of human life. From the dawn of creation, stories have been part of who we are. We love them, and we never seem to get enough.

Have you ever stopped to ask yourself *why*? *Why* are stories so treasured? Why do we hold our breath through an epic tale, ache at the hero's loss, or cheer as they triumph? Why do children — before they even understand all the words —delight in hearing a story read aloud? Why has humanity been drawn to storytelling for as long as we've existed? And why is it that we watch fictional characters walk through impossible trials with hope, yet when we face our own hardships, we often sink into hopelessness?

These are the questions we'll explore in this book. I believe the answer is both profound and divine. What's more? The answer is written on the human heart by our Creator from the very beginning.

Stories are in Our DNA

It's my firm belief that stories are so cherished because they've been written into our very DNA by the Creator Himself. God is the first and most excellent Author. He made everything: from the tiniest atom with its intricate design, to the towering peaks of the Himalayas, to the mind-blowing galaxies of outer space(many of which are still *undiscovered*). His creativity is endless, and it hasn't stopped! God is still creating —every day, in every person.

Where does He pour all that Creator-powered creativity? Into *writing*. God is the ultimate Author, crafting stories more beautiful and breathtaking than anything human imagination could produce. Have you ever read a book or watched a movie and wondered, *"How did they even think of that plot twist?"* Guess what? God writes even better stories than that.

The beauty of our Author-God is that He doesn't tell stories just to be creative or make a career of it. Storytelling is His nature. His stories are alive and active, with characters (us!) who have the free will to cooperate with Him or rebel and try to write our own stories. *We* are His stories, and His love for us is the very foundation of every plotline He creates.

For each of us, God is weaving a personal story with one goal: to draw us closer to Him and to align us with His will. In His grace and sovereignty, He works behind the scenes as the Master Author, shaping beautiful stories of growth, transformation, and redemption. As Paul writes, God wants to move us *"from one degree of glory to another"* (2 Corinthians 3:18). He never intends for us to stay the same. So let's toss out the false idea that "God loves me just the way I am." Yes, His love meets us where we are, but He doesn't leave us there. His goal is to make us more like Christ—newer, stronger, more radiant, and sanctified—until we reflect *His* image. That's the story He's writing, and it's worth every plot twist.

God's Stories vs. Our Preferences

God's stories aren't all warm and fuzzy like some modern "pastors" might suggest. The God of the Bible often uses challenging – even heart-wrenching—stories to transform His servants into who they need to be for His greatest purposes. *They may not be the stories we would choose, but His outcomes are always far greater than anything we could imagine.* He also follows a clear, specific process for moving His people from glory to glory, something I'll explore in the next chapter with plenty of Biblical examples.

Please hear my heart: this book is not meant to discourage you. In fact, it's the opposite. I want to share this revelation to fill you with the hope that no matter what you're facing right now, you can live out the truth that James wrote: "*Consider it pure joy, my brothers and sisters, whenever you face trials of many kinds… because you know that the testing of your faith produces perseverance. Let perseverance finish its work so that you may be mature and complete, not lacking anything*" (James 1:2-4). Pure joy in trials? Yes! Of any kind. You might be thinking, "How is that even possible? I didn't sign up for the various-trials-of-many-kinds part of Christianity!" But if you've picked up this book, my guess is that you've found yourself in an unexpected story and you're looking for answers. I hope to offer you those answers, or, at the very least, the strength to endure.

Though Pastor Jenni and I have lived very different lives, we've both faced trials of many kinds: deep pain, loss, betrayal, and unanswered questions. In some ways, we're still in those trenches. Yet we've learned this: no matter the circumstances, God's will is perfect. He is always sovereign. He is never wrong. And He is never absent. Just as David said in Psalm 139:

> "*Where can I go from your Spirit? Where can I flee from your presence? If I go up to the heavens, you are there; if I make my bed in the depths, you are there. If I rise on the wings of the dawn, if I settle on the far side of the sea, even there your hand will guide me, your right hand will hold me fast. If I say, "Surely the darkness will hide me and the light become night around me, even the darkness will not be dark to you; the night will shine like the day, for darkness is as light to you*" (Psalm 139:7-12, NIV).

Chelsea's Story

When I was growing up, I had a vivid imagination. As a kid, that meant inventing epic characters (my best friend and I called some of them "Poopski Bobs") and making up elaborate adventures for them. As I got older, my imagination shifted toward the perfect life I thought I'd have: land my dream job right out of college, buy a house, get married at 23, have my first child, a boy, at 24, then two more kids in the following years.

I'd serve the Lord faithfully, my children would grow up loving Him, and my husband would look and act just as I'd pictured. Life would be perfect.

It didn't turn out that way. Shocking, I know. I grew up in a strong Christian home with wonderful parents, but in high school, temptation found me. Insecurity about my looks, pride in my accomplishments, fear of rejection, and a craving for affirmation all left me vulnerable. By college, the added freedom only made it worse. By my junior year, at 21, I was partying, drinking, smoking weed, and sleeping around — nothing like the life I'd envisioned. I was drowning in sin, which eventually led to being sexually assaulted. I couldn't find my way out, and the cycle of sin carried into my young adult years.

In 2017, at 25, those choices led me into a terrible marriage with a dangerous man. Behind closed doors, I felt trapped and unprotected, with no one I thought I could turn to. It was my breaking point. Sitting alone in my house, I realized I had two paths: surrender to the abuse and become a shell of a person, or throw myself at the feet of Jesus and cry out for deliverance.

I chose Jesus. My faith became real. I prayed constantly for my marriage until March, 2020, in the early days of Covid lockdowns, when everything collapsed. I broke. I fled with my 13-month-old daughter and a single bag, finally telling my parents the truth. I began the divorce process. By 29, I was a divorced single mom, feeling like a failure who had wrecked not only her life but her child's as well.

The Lord began healing me from PTSD and the trauma of my first marriage, slowly rebuilding my trust in Him. Shortly after the divorce, God brought an amazing man into my life, and we married. Life began to feel "normal" again — not the old normal, but a new one. I was still broken and healing, but more mature and grounded in my faith. God used the darkness of my first marriage to draw me into deeper devotion to Him.

Since marrying Joshua in 2021, I've faced both fresh trials and moments of restoration, some of which I'll share in this book. But I wanted you to have this backdrop, a glimpse of my story, before meeting my pastor, mentor, and friend Pastor Jenni. She's been a steady guide through my healing, my second marriage, and yes, she's listened to plenty of my whining, too. Her wisdom has been a gift, and I'm excited for you to meet her and hear some of her story.

Jennifer's Story

I, Jenni, am a rainbow child. Before I was born, my mother miscarried a baby. Due to medical intervention, the miscarriage wreaked such havoc in her body that she hemorrhaged for six months. The counsel from her doctor was that, if she got pregnant again, she would most likely not be able to carry the baby to full term. My life was born from loss and grief. The sobering truth is that, had that child lived, I would never have existed. But that wasn't the only piece of my beginning. My life also began as a miracle and a mystery of God's mercy. Even my birth was a battle as the umbilical cord was wrapped around my neck. Yet, through every breath since, the Lord has gently reminded me: *"You have no idea what I've done to get you here."* That truth has shaped my heart to live in surrender, knowing that every part of my story is His design.

As a child, I carried a great deal of responsibility as the oldest of our home's "second set" of children. At eleven, a fall during a youth game triggered a difficult journey with epilepsy. This health condition became an unseen battle that changed everything. My battle with epilepsy would influence my life for *decades* to come. However, epilepsy would also open the door to future ministry growth.

At thirteen, through a family conflict and dealing with deep feelings of rejection, I encountered God personally for the first time. After one particular argument with my brother, I remember kneeling in the living room of our family home, feeling as if my head rested in Jesus' lap. I realized I had found a best friend in Him. Soon after, I felt drawn to the piano, which opened the door to worship.

At the young age of seventeen, I married Brad. I began working in a funeral home, surrounded by death and grief, while my husband and I served as youth pastors at our church. At twenty-one, the epilepsy began impacting my body more and more. I endured hundreds of seizures during my pregnancy with our first child, and I was diagnosed with hormone-induced epilepsy. Despite fear and medical uncertainty, God preserved both me and our baby girl, Jacque.

After Jacque's birth, my body stopped cycling for years, and I grieved infertility. A decade later, against all odds, a pregnancy test came back positive. Through nine months of shaky faith, God assured me, *"You are healed."* When our second daughter, Jessikah, was born, she was perfectly healthy—a living promise of restoration.

In 2001, while health issues continued to rage on, God called us to pioneer a church. In this process, I remember the Lord promising to train me in "the school of the Holy Spirit." The Lord would place me in positions of growth in front of the eyes of many. He walked me through seasons of humility and sanctification that were less than private. Since then, my growth in leadership, worship, and faith has unfolded publicly—every lesson learned in full view.

The years that followed were marked by both miracles and hardship. The medication used to control seizures had damaged my bone density, my teeth, and my jaw, leading to multiple surgeries and stage 4 osteoporosis. Then, in 2018, while leading worship, I suddenly damaged my voice. This caused a long season of unsurety for me emotionally, spiritually, and physically. I later underwent several vocal and oral surgeries. Yet even in that loss, God redirected me. In the loss of my voice, He deepened my piano skill, prophetic ministry, and passion for mentoring other worshipers.

More recently, my family has faced heartbreaking loss: my oldest brother's suicide during the COVID shutdowns and, two years later, my brother Ben's sudden death in a car accident. Through every tragedy, God has remained faithful. Many prophetic words spoken over my life took years (and some took decades) to be fulfilled. But I have learned to yield to His timing, trusting that even in the waiting, His story for my life is still being written, one surrendered day at a time.

Desensitized: A Quick Note

In today's hyper-connected world, we've grown a bit numb to the hardships others face. We can hear the powerful stories of saints, heroes, and martyrs of the faith, respect them in the moment, and then quickly move on – unchanged and unchallenged. The impact of their testimony gets dulled. Yet when our own trials come, we often respond with shock, anger, or even sin, forgetting the very examples we've admired.

Too often, we either downplay or overly spiritualize these figures. We downplay their stories by thinking, "They couldn't have handled what I'm going through," or, "That was common back then; they were used to that kind of trial." On the other hand, we sometimes put them on a pedestal, as if they had a superhuman faith that made them immune to struggle. Both of these approaches to these complex stories are wrong. Instead, we should approach these stories to learn from them, be encouraged by them, and let their faith fuel our own perseverance in the journey God has set before us.

This book is meant to walk with you in your own journey and to help you draw strength and wisdom from the Biblical heroes and founders of our faith. You'll see how they faced trials of many kinds, where they responded faithfully, and where they stumbled. I aim to help you understand why I believe God often writes our stories in ways we don't fully comprehend and to examine how we typically respond when trials occur. Through Scripture and the lessons God has revealed to us personally, we'll share how to move beyond our natural, human reactions and instead respond with faith, humility, and submission to Him.

To do that, we first need to look at the framework God so often uses in His stories. This framework is a timeless pattern you've likely seen in books and movies without even realizing it.

CHAPTER 2

What Makes a Good Story?

Have you ever read a book or watched a movie and walked away confused or unimpressed, thinking, "What did I just waste my time on?" Some stories fall flat and leave us wondering *What?* On the other hand, there are timeless, epic tales the whole world seems to love — *Star Wars, The Lord of the Rings, The Hunger Games, Pride and Prejudice, Hamlet,* and more — stories that capture hearts for generations. So, what makes some stories unforgettable while others quickly fade away? That "it" factor comes down to a specific plot pattern called **The Hero's Journey**, a term coined by literary scholar Joseph Campbell.

Now (Chelsea here), before I married Joshua and became a homeschool mom, I taught English and Creative Writing in public high school for six years. It was during my graduate studies and in teaching my students that I discovered (and fell in love with) The Hero's Journey. As a lifelong "words person," finally understanding why certain stories resonated so deeply was a lightbulb moment for me.

As my walk with the Lord deepened, primarily through seasons of intense trial, God began revealing to me divine truths tucked inside my love for The Hero's Journey. These are the truths we'll be sharing with you in this book.

So, bear with me as I get a little nerdy in this chapter. I'll give you a brief, clear explanation of what The Hero's Journey is and how this story structure is woven into our very DNA by the Creator. Don't skip this chapter thinking it's just literary theory! It's fundamental to understanding the rest of the book. I promise to keep it concise while still giving you the essentials.

The Hero with a Thousand Faces

Joseph Campbell, a literature professor at Sarah Lawrence College (New York) from 1934 to 1972, spent years studying mythological stories from across time, cultures, and nations. In his research, he began to notice a recurring story pattern—a shared story arc of character growth and transformation. He called this pattern the *monomyth*, or "The Hero's Journey." Campbell eventually compiled his findings into his book, *The Hero with a Thousand Faces* (1949), a work that has since influenced countless literary scholars, educators, authors, and story-lovers like me. His gift wasn't *inventing* the pattern but *identifying, naming, and organizing* it in a way that helped others see what had been there all along.

Campbell didn't *create* The Hero's Journey, just as Newton didn't *create* gravity. This plot structure has been part of humanity's storytelling since the beginning: in oral traditions, on chiseled stone tablets, on Egyptian papyrus, on Greek scrolls, and on the printed page. This story pattern permeates time and cultures because God Himself authored it, weaving it into the very DNA of humanity. That's why we're drawn to it! It's familiar to our souls because it comes from our Creator.

Before I dive into the details, a quick note: as followers of Jesus, I believe *He* is the only *true* Hero—the ultimate "Knight in shining armor," if you will. In this book, we'll still use the word *hero* in the literary sense, meaning the protagonist or main character of a story. Just keep in mind that while we'll explore many heroes, Jesus is the perfect fulfillment of this journey, and we'll see later how His life mirrors this divine pattern.

A Twelve-Step Story Structure

The Hero's Journey follows twelve steps that move the main character from their "normal world" into a new, "different world," where they grow, change, and emerge transformed. While specific stories may vary slightly, this twelve-step framework remains consistent across most stories.

Even the fact that Campbell identified *twelve* core stages is no accident. Our God is a God of order and precision, never doing anything by mistake. In Scripture, the number twelve symbolizes *God's power, heavenly authority, perfect governmental foundation, and completion.* This number is reflected in creation as a type and shadow of the perfection we find in the heavenly throneroom. And it appears often — far more often than we might realize. Biblical numerology, the symbolism of numbers in the Bible, is actually something I very much enjoy studying in my own Bible study times. According to BibleStudy.org, the number twelve is used 189 times in Scripture. Here are just a *few* key examples:

- Twelve generations from Noah's son, Shem, to Jacob.
- The twelve sons of Jacob who became the twelve tribes of Israel. These twelve are also seen in Joseph's two dreams with the stars and the sheaves of wheat.
- God's command for twelve loaves of unleavened bread to remain in the temple each week.
- Solomon's twelve officers governing Israel.
- Jesus called twelve disciples, later giving them the power and authority to build His church (Matthias replacing Judas Iscariot after Jesus' resurrection).
- Twelve mentions of Passover in the entire Bible.
- Twelve minor prophet books.
- In Revelation, twelve groups of twelve thousand are set apart for the Lord, the woman crowned with twelve stars, the New Jerusalem's twelve gates of pearl, and two sets of twelve elders around God's throne.
- Even creation reflects this design: twelve months in Earth's orbit, and two sets of twelve hours marking each day.

Clearly, God values numerical consistency and symbolism, and He has written this twelve-step pattern of growth into the hearts of His most beloved creation: humanity.

Defining the 12 Steps of The Hero's Journey Story Archetype

I'm going to give you a brief overview of each step in The Hero's Journey. Some of Campbell's titles may sound unusual, but they're the terms he used. Later, I'll explain how God uses these steps not just in literature, but in real, raw, God-written life stories. For this overview, I'll use a non-Biblical example, the popular children's movie *The Lion King*, to illustrate each stage. In later chapters, I'll show you how these same steps play out in Scripture.

1. **The Ordinary World:** Life before the journey.

Everything is normal, and the hero is content to live their life as it is. The hero is oblivious to the trials that lie ahead.

Example: Simba, as a carefree cub, plays in the grasslands with his father.

2. **Call to Action:** Something happens that draws the hero from their "normal."

An unexpected event or invitation draws the hero out of their routine. This could be a life situation that confronts the normal circumstances of life or an actual invitation from someone or something that calls the hero into something new.

Example: Scar plants seeds of doubt in Simba's courage. Scar tempts Simba to explore the Elephant Graveyard to prove his bravery.

3. **Refusal of the Call:** Fear creeps in.

Although the hero may not realize it, they hesitate due to fear, insecurity, or defiance. Typically, fear (and personal insecurity rooted in fear of failure) is the most common reason for refusing the call.

Example: In the Graveyard, danger and the mockery from the Hyenas shake Simba's confidence. Shortly after, Simba apologizes to his father and begins to feel as if he may not be able to be brave at all.

4. **Meeting the Mentor:** Wisdom arrives to help guide the hero.

When fear swells within the hero and cripples their forward movement, a mentor usually comes alongside to provide the wisdom, guidance, support, or encouragement needed to get started on their journey.

Example: Mufasa talks to Simba about the source of true bravery and that true bravery isn't reckless. This advice comes full circle at the end of the movie when he needs to confront Scar.

5. **Crossing the First Threshold:** The hero steps into the unknown world.

The hero—either willingly or unwillingly—leaves their comfort zone. This is the true beginning of the journey away from the "normal world." This portion is usually physical, emotional, spiritual, or a combination of two or three of these.

Example: After Mufasa's murder, Simba flees into unknown exile. His journey takes place in a physical setting, but is also immensely emotional, as he battles the shame he feels about his father's death.

6. **Tests, Allies, Enemies:** Navigating the New World.

Now facing an entirely new world and circumstances, the hero now has to traverse various challenges - who can they trust, where should they go, how can they be successful, when will these challenges ever end, and more. Throughout this part of the journey, the hero will encounter allies/friends and enemies, and begin to face various trials and battles. This section of The Hero's Journey is usually the most substantial portion of the journey. What takes place in this part of the story typically grows and matures the hero—sometimes without them even realizing it—preparing them to encounter their biggest battle (the "Ordeal").

Example: Simba gets lost in the desert, meets Timon and Pumbaa, learns jungle life, reconnects with Nala, discovers the Pridelands' plight, and meets Rafiki. All of these pieces of his journey help him heal from the pain and betrayal of his past.

7. **Approach to the Inmost Cave:** Confronting the core fear.

This typically forces the hero to come face-to-face with their biggest fear (which is usually revealed in the "Refusal of the Call"). This will sometimes involve reflecting or speaking with their mentor, or even feeling a backslide deep into their fear, before they remember all that they have learned in their journey thus far.

Example: Nala reveals the status of the Pridelands and urges Simba to return as king. His fear of failure and deep-seated doubts are further confronted when Rafiki finds him and tells Simba how much of his father, the brave Mufasa, is hiding within Simba's own heart. Simba has a vision of his father, who tells him to "Remember who you are." This is when the wisdom of Mufasa from "Meeting the Mentor" resurfaces and begins to really challenge Simba's self-assessment of himself.

8. **Ordeal:** The hero's biggest test yet!

This is when the hero must draw on everything they have learned thus far in their journey and face their biggest fear. The hero faces a symbolic *death* and emerges reborn as a new version of themselves; their fears, although still present, have been broken and bridled. This experience gives them the strength, power, or insight to fulfill their goal or destiny.

Example: Simba encounters this when he decides to return to the Pridelands after his father's vision. Simba puts his "Hakuna Matata" apathy to death, choosing to confront Scar and reclaim his place as king.

9. **Reward (also called "Seizing the Sword"):** Gaining the reward from all the hardships.

The hero receives a tangible or intangible reward as they walk through their Ordeal. This will sometimes appear as a new ability, emotional state, or equipment necessary for quest completion. Regardless of the story, there is always a "prize" that the hero has earned by facing and overcoming their biggest fear.

Example: Simba recognizes that he has the courage that he has constantly desired. He has faced his emotional turmoil and emerged with a new-found identity and bravery.

10. **The Road Back:** Returning to face the past.

The hero isn't safe yet, and trials are still coming. However, the hero is equipped differently (with the "reward") to handle these trials of the Road Back. Armed with new strength, the hero heads home. The prize they have won will always help them on this road.

Example: Simba's return to the Pridelands reveals a confident leader – by the way he carries himself, moves, and even speaks to Scar. He is no longer the frightened cub who fled years ago.

11. **Resurrection:** The final battle.

This is the climax of the story, as the hero must face the final challenge of this journey. The hero emerges as a new, resurrected version of themself. When this final battle is finished, the result is an entirely new version of the hero, with new maturity, strength, wisdom, and understanding.

Example: On Pride Rock, when Scar confesses to the murder of Mufasa, the greatest battle of Simba's life begins. This battle is far beyond Simba's abilities, but with the newfound identity and bravery from the vision of his father, he can overcome the final battle. Simba defeats Scar, saving the kingdom.

12. **Return with the Elixir:** The hero emerges into a NEW normal.

The hero returns to their old "normal" world transformed with a new identity, maturity, strength, or abilities. The hero is usually met with celebration, gratitude, deeper self-realization, or the end of strife. Whatever the outcome, three key elements generally accompany the hero's return: ***change, success, and proof of the journey.***

Example: Simba ascends Pride Rock as king. He has changed significantly, which is symbolized by the birth of his and Nala's cub.

I hope this has helped you better understand The Hero's Journey and see how easily this plot structure applies to real life. I used *The Lion King* because it's so well-known, but there are endless examples. As we move through this book, we'll look at your own story—whether it's a past journey or the one you're in now—and identify where the Lord has you in His journey. Maybe you're at the beginning, stuck in Refusal of the Call. Perhaps you're in the thick of the Ordeal, unsure how to move forward. Or maybe you can look back on significant seasons and clearly see each step aligning with God's bigger plan. Wherever you are, I hope you find encouragement and know you are not alone. Many saints and sinners have walked this same road before us. The most encouraging part, however, is this: the Creator has chosen a story designed specifically for *your* growth, success, and testimony—one that ends with a transformed you, reflecting more of His image.

Identifying The Hero's Journey: Where have you seen this story archetype?

The Hero's Journey appears in thousands of stories across history. It's in the ancient epics, like *The Odyssey, The Epic of Gilgamesh, Beowulf,* and in classics like *Jane Eyre, The Chronicles of Narnia, Great Expectations, The Inferno, Macbeth,* and *Hamlet.* It continues in modern works like *The Lion King, Rocky, The Lord of the Rings, Star Wars,* and *The Hunger Games.* The list could go on and on! Give me an epic story, and I can likely map it to The Hero's Journey.

But here's the "meat and potatoes": this isn't just a clever literary device. We see The Hero's Journey woven throughout Scripture, which isn't a fictional example! They are real, God-written stories. And that's the evidence of His fingerprints on the very design of this archetype.

We can clearly trace these twelve steps in the lives of Noah, Gideon, Elijah, Esther, Ruth, and Daniel. Each began in an ordinary life, received a call from God, endured trials, and emerged changed—completing their mission. And that's just a handful of examples. Page after page, God has given us real accounts of His people walking this same path so we could learn, grow, and be encouraged. In the coming chapters, we'll explore some of the most vivid examples: Job, Abraham, Joseph, Moses, Joshua, King David, and the Apostle Paul.

The Hero's Journey is written on every human heart because it's GOD'S story – a pattern He uses in the sanctifying, growing, and maturing of His children. It resonates deep within us because it mirrors creation, redemption, and transformation—from one degree of glory to the next. Praise God!

CHAPTER 3

Great Value at a Great Cost

Chapter by Pastor Jennifer Neuschwander

Every believer's life is a story under construction. Some days feel like smooth, steady progress, while others feel like collapse—a vessel cracked, a dream shattered, a plan that didn't hold. Yet in both the beauty and the brokenness, there is a consistent truth: God is at work.

And God works in ways we will never understand. He even tells us this much through the prophet Isaiah, when He said, *"For my thoughts are not your thoughts, neither are your ways my ways, declares the LORD. For as the heavens are higher than the earth, so are my ways higher than your ways and my thoughts than your thoughts"* (Isaiah 55:8–9). Oftentimes, His ways can seem difficult, complicated, and even sometimes beyond our human understanding!

The Bible is filled with accounts of God's hand working in the lives of His people, and some of them seem downright mean. These stories really challenge our man-centered theology that teaches us that "God is always nice" and that "life gets better when you're following Jesus" (just ask Joseph or Job how that "theology" worked out in their lives). The reality is that God's handiwork takes many different forms, but his most significant works look the strangest to our human intellect. In those most difficult stories, God is sowing, planting, cultivating, pruning, and unveiling His greatest harvest and sweetest fruits.

To help you better understand how God's story-writing process fits into the lives of His people, I, Jenni, have two analogies to share. Both of these have Scriptural roots (with parables from Jesus to back them up), and I believe God has really opened my eyes to deeper truths hidden within Scripture *and* even within creation itself. One is the potter at his wheel, patiently shaping, pressing, crushing, and molding His clay into a vessel of purpose. The other analogy I want to share with you is that of a pearl forming inside an oyster, where a wound slowly transforms into beauty. Another is Jesus' parable of the treasure hidden in a field. It was a treasure so valuable that it was worth giving up everything to obtain.

These images remind us that our value and destiny are not self-made. We are not the Potter, nor do we create our own worth. We are shaped, covered, and redeemed by God Himself.

The Potter and the Clay

In the book of Jeremiah, there is a beautiful real-life example that God reveals to the prophet. He sent Jeremiah to the potter's workshop. We see this situation take place in this passage: *"Then the word of the LORD came to me, saying: 'O house of Israel,* **can I not do with you as this potter?'** *says the LORD. 'Look,* **as the clay is in the potter's hand, so are you in My hand**, *O house of Israel!'"* (Jeremiah 18:5-6). When God wanted to make His relationship with Israel clear, He sent Jeremiah to watch a potter at work. It kind of seems a bit strange at first. Jeremiah saw the potter's vessel being marred, crushed, and pressed in the artist's hands. Yet, no matter how marred the clay became, the potter did not discard it. He did not throw away the clay because of its flaws. Instead, he continued working and reshaped it into something new.

This is God's heart toward His people, toward us. He has absolute sovereignty. He may pluck up or plant, tear down or build (like He continues to explain in Jeremiah 18:7–10). Yet His sovereignty is not cold or mechanical. It is personal. It is purposeful. It is beautiful. And it has been this way since the beginning of Creation. Go back to Genesis with me:

"The LORD God formed the man of dust from the ground and breathed into his nostrils the breath of life, and the man became a living creature" (Genesis 2:7). The Creator Himself stepped away from Heaven and onto His Earth to form – by hand! – His most beloved ones: humanity. From the beginning, He was a Potter.

Here is a profound paradox regarding our God: He is unchanging in His nature, yet responsive in His dealings. He never changes *who He is*, but He does *respond to who we are* with both beauty, tenderness, and intimate knowledge of who we are. And so the message of the potter is not just about God's authority. It is also about His grace and mercy. **He never discards or abandons us, His chosen lumps of clay. Even when we become marred by the process, if we stay submitted to His hands, He remakes what is marred.** And, sometimes, He mars what He has made to remake it into something even better. There is safety in the hands of the Potter. It is not to be feared or to feel powerless. Your life is not an accident. Your heartbreaks and tragedies are not accidents. Your story is not beyond repair. The hands that formed galaxies are steady enough to reshape your cracks.

The Mystery of the Pearl

If the analogy of the potter shows us God's sovereignty, the pearl shows us the precious worth He places on our lives – the good, the bad, and the ugly. Even more than that, God values our pain, our trials, and our heartbreaks. He uses those moments more than anything else to shape us into priceless gems in His eyes.

Proverbs 8:10–11 tells us: *"Receive my instruction, and not silver; and knowledge rather than choice gold. For wisdom is better than rubies or pearls, and all the things one may desire are not to be compared with her."* In ancient times, pearls were among the most costly of treasures. They were pursued by kings, traded for fortunes, and adorned royalty. Unlike a diamond carved from stone, a pearl is the only precious gem born from a living creature.

When a grain of sand or a parasite wounds an oyster, God created this unique creature to do something exceptional and beautiful. The oyster responds to the irritant or wound by covering it with nacre – more commonly known as "mother-of-pearl." Over time, layer upon layer, what began as an injury becomes something luminous and priceless. Natural pearls of great worth are rare—one in every 10,000 oysters! And the most valuable, South Sea pearls, require years of formation in the cleanest, most pristine waters. They are fragile in process yet radiant in outcome.

The beauty of the pearl is a living parable of God's redemption. We each encounter hardships in this life. Those trials – the irritant of the oyster – are the scars of sin. We are pierced by pain and wounded by life. Yet God does not discard us. Instead, He covers us with His righteousness, grace upon grace, until what was once broken begins to shine. Our pain, irritants, and wounds are remade into something beautiful and priceless. Paul captures this sentiment especially well when he said, *"Your life is hidden with Christ in God"* (Colossians 3:3). The pearl's worth lies not in its origin as a wound but in its repurposing and beautification. Likewise, our worth lies not in our flawless, empty beginnings, but in Christ's flawless covering of every pain we encounter.

The Pearl of Great Price and the Treasure in the Field

If you're wondering about the Biblical significance of the pearl, Jesus pointed directly to this when He told the parable of the pearl: *"The kingdom of heaven is like a merchant seeking fine pearls, who, when he had found one pearl of great price, went and sold all that he had and bought it"* (Matthew 13:45–46). The parable can be read in two dimensions. First, it can be interpreted as seeing Christ as the pearl. We should sell all to gain Him. On the flip side, God gives the parable a secondary meaning: we are also the pearl. God is the man who sold all, laying down His very life, to purchase us – His priceless treasures. The rarity, beauty, and costliness of the pearl point us to the immeasurable value God places on His people.

Just before this, Jesus gave the parable of the hidden treasure: *"The kingdom of heaven is like treasure hidden in a field, which a man found and hid; and for joy over it he goes and sells all that he has and buys that field"* (Matthew 13:44). Here, we see a parable of similar type to that of the pearl! Both parables end the same way: with someone selling *everything*. Why? Because the treasure is of such surpassing worth that nothing else compares. Both interpretations of these parables hold tremendous weight. Christ gave everything – through pain and immense agony – to gain those whom He cherished, so we are to endure whatever comes our way to gain Christ, the most priceless of treasures. Can we take a moment to recognize the sheer immenseness of these two quick but powerful parables? Wow.

As Augustine wrote: *"You have made us for Yourself, and our heart is restless until it rests in You."*

The Potter's Key Theme: God's Sovereignty and Mercy

The image of the potter that Jeremiah gives us reminds us that our lives are in the hands of a holy, sovereign God. I'll repeat it: being within the hands of our Potter and on His wheel is not something to be feared! It's actually a beautiful place to be, an analogy of just how involved and personally invested our God is in each of our lives. Just as clay yields to the skilled hands of the potter, so God is shaping each of us according to His purposes (Jeremiah 18:6). The same sentiment is given later in Jeremiah when God said, *"For I know the plans I have for you, declares the LORD, plans for welfare and not for evil, to give you a future and a hope"* (Jeremiah 29:11). Even when our lives are marred by pain, hardships, mistakes, or broken circumstances, God's mercy remakes us because His plan is to give us a future and hope!

Paul reminds us further that we are *"God's workmanship, created in Christ Jesus for good works"* (Ephesians 2:10). Despite being hundreds of years apart, Paul and Jeremiah emphasize the same truth: the Potter isn't only in the business of *simply shaping us.* Instead, He does the shaping in us for a purpose that is *good and eternal* – even when we don't understand His methods. The picture of the Potter teaches us to trust God—no matter the circumstances—whether we feel cracked, imperfect, falling apart, or ready to give up. In those shaky times, God's hands are steady. This is when He does His best work. His intentions are always perfect, and His shaping is always intentional. The best part is that He will never give up on us.

The Pearl's Key Theme: God's Grace in Transformation

The pearl illustrates the beauty of God's transformative grace. His transformative process is founded on the sureness of His grace. This is also a key theme that you will find woven throughout this entire book. For the pearl, what began as an irritating wound inside the oyster, slowly started the process of redemption. Layer upon layer of mother-of-pearl came upon the irritant until it became a gem of great value.

In the same way, God's grace covers our pain, wounds, failures, trials, and weaknesses, gradually forming Christlike beauty in our character. He doesn't leave the painful irritation unaddressed. He also doesn't *remove* the irritant. Instead, He *uses the irritant* to create something beautiful. Paul compares this hidden work to a spiritual transformation: *"We all, with unveiled face, beholding the glory of the Lord, are being transformed into the same image **from one degree of glory to another**"* (2 Corinthians 3:18). Just as the pearl is rare and precious, the beauty God creates in our Hero's Journey is costly and divine, a testimony to His loving care and patience.

The Treasure: The Surpassing Worth of Christ

Finally, the treasure reminds us of the incomparable value of Christ Himself and the beauty of the way He values us. This is astounding to me. In two parables, Jesus compared the Kingdom of Heaven to both a treasure hidden in a field and a pearl of great price (Matthew 13:44–46), illustrating that nothing in the world can compare with knowing Him. Imagine: the immeasurably priceless Savior of the World and Son of God values each of us tremendously! This is echoed throughout God's Word. Paul wrote that knowing Christ surpasses everything else: *"I count everything as loss because of the surpassing worth of knowing Christ Jesus my Lord"* (Philippians 3:8). The treasure image challenges us to reorient our hearts: to sell all in pursuit of Christ, to value His presence above every worldly possession, and to recognize that our eternal reward is found in Him alone. Why? Because He did that very thing for each of us in His sacrifice on the cross.

These images are beautifully woven throughout Scripture and Creation. They are not random! They are designed.

- **The Potter** shows us God's sovereignty and mercy—He can remake what is marred.

- **The Pearl** shows us God's grace in transformation—He covers our wounds until beauty emerges.

- **The Treasure** shows us the surpassing worth of Christ—nothing compares with having Him.

Together, they tell us this: God will allow us to walk through the hardships of this life to grow, shape, mold, and transform us. The best part? This is where His most significant value is made in us. This is where we are transformed from *"from one degree of glory to another"* (2 Corinthians 3:18). This is the most beautiful reward we could receive from the hand of our Great Potter.

The Potter reminds us that failures and trials are not final. God is in the business of remaking any piece of artwork that is marred. The Pearl is a picture that teaches us that our wounds, when covered by His grace, can become radiant and transformative for His glory. The parable of the Treasure stands as a testimony that nothing in this world compares with the surpassing worth of knowing Christ. *Nothing!* When we look at these analogies together, both real and fictional, we can see the clear message that God is calling us to rest in His strong hands, to trust His strong hands, and to treasure Him above all else. With that in mind, in this section, take a moment to reflect personally on how these truths are shaping your own journey with Him.

Self-Reflection

1. **The Potter** – Where do you feel "marred," pressed, or broken right now? How might God be reshaping you instead of discarding you?

2. **The Pearl** – What irritants or wounds in your life has God begun covering with His grace? Can you trace His work of transformation through seasons of pain?

3. **The Treasure** – What would it look like for you to "sell all" for the sake of Christ? What distractions, comforts, or false treasures compete for your heart?

4. How does seeing yourself as clay in His hands *and* as His pearl of great price reshape your understanding of your worth?

Closing Prayer

Father, I yield myself to Your loving hands. Thank You that You do not discard me when I am marred, but that You remake me for Your purpose. Thank you for the pressing, crushing, and molding. I see now that those moments of pain and hardship in my life are opportunities for you to transform me into your image. Thank You that You cover my wounds with grace, transforming my weakness into beauty. Thank you for not abandoning me to the pain. Thank you for not wasting my hardships and trials! Thank You that You treasure me so profoundly that You gave all to make me Yours. Teach me to treasure You above all else. Show me how I can give it all for you! Shape me, cover me, and fill me until my life reflects Your glory. In Jesus' name, Amen.

PART 2

What Does This Look Like in the Lives of Significant People in the Bible?

Over the following chapters, I (Chelsea) will dive into the lives of men in the Bible who played a significant role in accomplishing God's will. While many others in the Bible also walked The Hero's Journey, covering them all would make this book far too long. I've chosen a select few men from Biblical history:

1. Job: Trusting the Author in the Darkest Chapter

2. Abraham: Walking by Faith When the Map is Blank

3. Joseph: From Dreams to Detours

4. Moses: When the Wilderness Becomes Holy Ground

5. Joshua: The Courage to Conquer

6. David: The Crown Forged in the Cave

7. The Apostle Paul: When Misplaced Zeal Meets Transforming Grace

For these seven men, each of their lives follows The Hero's Journey perfectly. For those wanting to more deeply understand how each of their stories fits into The Hero's Journey plotline, I have plotted out and placed them each in an Appendix at the end of the book. After these chapters, I hope to leave you with a strong understanding of how God has molded these men on the Potter's wheel and brought them into greater promise and destiny. We'll also challenge a common misconception often sold to new believers: that following Jesus instantly solves every problem and makes life smooth. There's a grain of truth in that, but if you asked Job or Joseph whether life became "hunky dory" when they followed God, they'd tell a different story.

Along the way, I hope to equip you with profound scriptural truths and practical tips to take from these men's lives and apply to your own personal journeys and struggles. This isn't just about giving you information – it's about equipping you to walk out your faith with resilience and trust. I want to provide you with as many practical resources as I can to help you get through the hardest seasons of your life. To help you do that, each chapter will close with a three-part reflection guide:

1. **Pause on the Path**: A short devotional thought that recaps the chapter's key idea and brings it to *your* heart's level.

2. **Putting It Into Practice**: Simple but concrete next steps you can take in the coming week to live out what you've studied, reflected on, and learned.

3. **Prayer for the Journey**: A short, Christ-centered prayer to help you offer the lesson back to God and to apply it to your life from a surrendered heart.

If you're an avid reader, it will be tempting to race through this section of the book. I encourage you to slow down—especially in Part 2 of the book. Spend a week or more in each chapter: read, reflect, answer the questions, and engage with the suggested Scriptures. I would encourage you to get a journal or notebook to accompany your journey through the rest of this book. Each chapter will end with opportunities for reflection and application with specific journal and prayer prompts. Recording your thoughts and answers will guide you in your understanding of the challenging truths presented in these pages. Don't rush the process; growth takes time.

Now that you know what's ahead, let's begin walking alongside some of the most remarkable men of God – men whose journeys helped shape our faith and the very pages of Scripture. Let's dive in!

CHAPTER 4

Job: Trusting the Author in the Darkest Chapter

Most people avoid the book of Job as if it were a spiritual horror story. I get it – I did too. As a kid, the thought terrified me; here's this man faithfully serving God, when suddenly it seems like God Almighty hands him over to Satan in some weird game of wits. *"Why would God do that?"* my young mind thought. *"That doesn't sound like the God I know!"* That question haunted me for years.

Over time, as I've grown in my faith and studied Job more in-depth, God has opened my eyes to the beauty in this book. Beneath the heartbreak, suffering, and confusion lies a profound example of how God works in mysterious and perfect ways—even when they don't make sense to us.

One of my favorite authors, introduced to me by Pastor Jenni, is Bob Sorge—a man of faith who has walked through his own Hero's Journey of trials, questions, and incredible spiritual fruit. Two of his books in particular have shaped my understanding of Job: *Pain, Perplexity, and Promotion* (1996) and *The Fire of Delayed Answers* (1999). I can't recommend them enough. Sorge's insight into Job's life is both challenging and transformative, offering a depth of understanding that lingers long after reading.

I'll draw on his research in this chapter, condensing the essence of his work into a much shorter form. My goal is to give you a fresh perspective on Job—one that may surprise you if you've always seen it as a "scary" book. If what you read here sparks your interest, Sorge's works are a great next step for digging deeper.

Job, the Oldest Book of the Bible

Job is one of the Bible's great enigmas! Its author is unknown, and its timeline is uncertain. Many Christians like to pass over this book like room-temperature asparagus that's been sitting out too long at the Thanksgiving buffet line! To the casual reader, the book of Job seems confusing, mean, unfair, and sort of whiny. Yet when we look more closely, Job's story is rich with timeless spiritual truth. As we spend the following pages diving into this man's journey, I hope you will see that Job's life holds tremendous sacred nuggets of wisdom that are important and applicable to our lives today.

Through reading and studying this book, I personally lean toward the view, shared by author Bob Sorge, that Job may be the first book of Scripture ever recorded. Since there is no definitive way to prove this idea, I have a few reasons to believe that the book of Job was the first book of the Bible. Two main clues point in this direction:

1. Lifespans of Early-Bible Men

Before the flood, people lived extraordinarily long lifespans, which gradually shortened afterward. Noah lived 950 years (Gen. 9:29), Shem 600 (Gen. 11:10–11), Arphaxad 438 (Gen. 11:12–13), Peleg 239 (Gen. 11:18–19), Abraham 175 (Gen. 25:7), Jacob 147 (Gen. 47:28), and Joseph 110 years (Gen. 50:26). Using the ages listed above, we could take a given age of a person living in early Bible times (say, an example person who lived for 200 years) and assess around the time period in which that person lived (a 200-year-old person would live approximately during the time after Noah's great-great grandson, Peleg, and Abraham).

Although Job's specific age isn't mentioned, there are some clues we can use to deduce the approximate age of Job. I have to credit Bob Sorge for his expert research, much of which I have reviewed and agreed with. The typical age for men to marry and begin families was around 30 years old (see Genesis 11:12-24). We know Job had ten adult children at the story's start (Job 1:2–3). Assuming he married at the typical age of 30 and his youngest child was about 30, with each sibling roughly a year apart, Job would have been at least 70 when his trials began. Another clue is given when his friends are called "very old" (Job 32:6), suggesting he may have been older still. After his ordeal, Job lived another 140 years (Job 42:16), placing his age at death at least 210 years old – consistent with post-flood but pre-Abrahamic lifespans, shortly after Noah's great-great-grandson, Peleg.

2. Absence of Abrahamic-Covenant References

Throughout the entire book of Job, there is no mention of Abraham, Isaac, Jacob, the covenant, Israel's slavery in Egypt, Moses, or the Law—events that dominate Genesis 12 through Deuteronomy 34. If Job lived *after* these events, such foundational history would almost certainly appear in his story as He scrambled to understand the hardship and gravity of what he was experiencing. Instead, the book reflects a pre-Abrahamic world where all people were Gentiles with equal access to God. Sorge notes: "Noah... Enoch... Melchizedek... Even Abraham was a Gentile" before God's covenant (Sorge, 1996).

Together, these clues suggest that Job's life occurred long before the patriarchs, making his story, what I believe, the earliest written Scripture. For a deeper dive, I highly recommend Sorge's *Pain, Perplexity, and Promotion*, which expands on this evidence in detail.

A Difficult Read

For most of my life, whenever hardship hit, I heard many Christian friends say, "It's an attack from the enemy!" and then we'd pray for God's favor and protection. Even now, at age 33, I hear friends lament: "I've been praying against this attack, and nothing's changing!" or "Why is God letting this happen?" Sometimes there's even a fiery *"Not today, Satan!"* with a full Pentecostal flair.

Now, these responses aren't necessarily bad or wrong. I've felt them and said them myself! However, these responses often miss a key truth: God, the Almighty Author, is always crafting a story and a testimony within His children to bring them from one degree of glory into another. The book of Job blows a Volkswagen-Bug-sized hole in the idea that "God doesn't let bad things happen to good people."

The story opens with Job—wealthy, respected, happy, and the father of ten adult children who seem to enjoy their dad's good fortune a little too much. We are told that Job actually recognizes his kids' inappropriate lifestyles and is seemingly embarrassed by it! He offers consistent sacrifices to the Lord to atone for the sins of his children (see Job 1:1-5). The scene then shifts to Heaven's throne room. Satan, that serpent of old, approaches the King on the throne, and we see a brief glimpse into the structure and etiquette of the courtroom of heaven. In a shocking turn of events, God Himself actually brings up Job's name (note that Satan wasn't the one who brought up Job) and challenges Satan with the faithful heart of Job:

> "Now there was a day when the sons of God came to present themselves before the LORD, and Satan also came among them. The LORD said to Satan, 'From where have you come?' Satan answered the LORD and said, 'From going to and fro on the earth, and from walking up and down on it.' And the LORD said to Satan, **'Have you considered my servant Job, that there is none like him on the earth, a blameless and upright man, who fears God and turns away from evil?'"** (Job 1:6-8).

Yikes. God essentially volunteers Job as the prize in a divine wager. Satan is granted permission to strip away nearly everything – his children, wealth, home, status – in moments. I can't even imagine the pain of that loss. What a horrific day for our real-life protagonist, Job.

From here, when many of us would be a puddle of tears on the ground, cursing God for the pain of this loss, Job does something astounding: he worships God. Job 1:20-22 shows us Job's response to the tragedy that hit him: "*Then Job arose and tore his robe and shaved his head and fell on the ground and worshiped. And he said, 'Naked I came from my mother's womb, and naked shall I return. The LORD gave, and the LORD has taken away; blessed be the name of the LORD.'*" This is actually the *first* mention of the Hebrew word for *worship* in the Bible! Job—despite the unimaginable grief—responds with **worship**. My deepest desire in this life is to reach a point of faith in God where I can respond to the worst heartache with worship.

But Satan isn't done. He argues that Job's worship is only because his health is still intact. God permits round two, this time allowing Job's body to be attacked Satan covers Job with painful sores. Despite his friends' harsh accusations, Job refuses to curse God. His wife, who also experienced the same amount of loss and grief herself, encourages Job to curse God! Hers and her husband's responses are absolute opposites: *"Then his wife said to him, 'Do you still hold fast your integrity? Curse God and die.' But he said to her, 'You speak as one of the foolish women would speak. Shall we receive good from God, and shall we not receive evil?' In all this, Job did not sin with his lips"* (Job 2:9-10). Let's slow down and read that last part again: *"Shall we receive good from God, and shall we not receive evil?"* That one line shatters much of the modern "sunshine and rainbows" gospel. Through chapters of friends insisting Job must have sinned, Job maintains his innocence, wrestles with his grief, and clings to God. Although we see him struggle through the absolute agony and suffering of his losses and infirmities, by the end of the book of Job, the Lord meets with Job face to face. We see God commend Job for his faithfulness, correct his thinking where needed, praise his faithfulness, and then restore him beyond imagination.

Now that we've walked through Job's life, I hope you can see the fingerprints of God's divine plotline woven throughout: normal life, call to action, meeting the mentor, trials and enemies, transformation, reward, and return. To get a complete outline of Job's story lined up with The Hero's Journey, see Appendix 1. Job's calamity lets us see how God uses this specific story arc to grow, mature, and sanctify Job – moving him from one degree of glory (as seen in Job 1:8 when God said about Job: *"Have you considered my servant Job, that there is none like him on the earth, a blameless and upright man, who fears God and turns away from evil?"*) to the next degree of glory, when God credits Job for being one of the three most righteous men on to live on earth in the book of Ezekiel (*"'Even if Noah, Daniel, and Job were in it, as I live,' declares the Lord GOD, 'they would deliver neither son nor daughter. They would deliver but their own lives by their righteousness"* Ezekiel 14:20). I recommend reading Job after you finish this chapter! You may see it in a whole new light.

As profound as the Book of Job is, it is still so often avoided. Why? Because it challenges our comfort theology and forces us to face the unsettling truth that God may allow sovereignly-designed seasons that look "evil" to us, yet are for our good. This true story forces us to come to terms with Job's question: *"Shall we receive good from God, and shall we not receive evil?"* Ugh. That's a tricky question, but it's a question that we hope to bring some answers to throughout the duration of this book.

Even if Job's story were the only example we had of God's transformative storytelling, it would be enough. But don't worry! We'll look at other men in Scripture who walked this same path in their own way. Although one of the most challenging stories in the Bible to read, Job's life serves as a vivid reminder that even in the most profound suffering, God can bring us out transformed, with a clearer view of ourselves and of Him.

Key Themes from the Life of Job

The book of Job is one of the richest and most theologically profound narratives in the Bible, a fitting way to begin the divinely inspired Word of God. His story, although difficult to understand on a surface level, tackles themes that are both beautiful and challenging! They really don't cater to a simple passing read. For each of the following themes from Job, each is filled with deep meaning and wisdom for our lives today. Here are the key Biblical themes found in the Book of Job:

1. Mystery of Suffering

The life of Job presents one of Scripture's most interesting explorations of suffering, faith, and divine mystery. Though blameless and upright (as seen in Job 1:1), Job still experiences devastating loss without apparent reason. This dismantles the ancient and modern theology that teaches "suffering is the result of personal sin." Instead, this narrative reveals to us that human beings often lack the perspective to understand God's purposes. Suffering, although usually impossible to understand, can be a beautiful mystery in which God chooses to grow and transform His children.

2. God's Sovereignty

From the very start, Job's story emphasizes God's sovereignty over creation, including Satan, nature, and human affairs. Even Satan cannot act in the world without God's divine permission. We also see God's sovereignty even in suffering. God remains in control even when events seem chaotic or unjust. This control doesn't mean that God offers immediate explanations – another brutal truth to come to terms with in the Book of Job.

3. Faith in the Midst of Darkness

One of the most inspiring pieces of Job's story is that he continues to seek God even when his circumstances are incomprehensible. His famous cry, *"Though he slay me, yet will I hope in him"* (Job 13:15), captures the raw honesty and endurance of *true* faith. His faith wasn't insincere or ignorant! He acknowledged his pain and suffering! He cried out regarding them. Although Job did not understand his suffering, still he refused to curse God. His laments were honest, from a heart that was experiencing the worst, most painful kinds of grief, but he continued to seek God. This reminds us today of an important truth from this theme: ***faith isn't the absence of questions; it is continuing to seek God amidst them.*** True faith persists even without answers.

4. Limit of Human Wisdom

In their attempts to "help," Job's friends operate on rigid theological *assumptions*, insisting that Job's suffering must be a punishment for sin. This demonstrates that human logic falls short of explaining God's ways. This reminds us today to constantly search the Scriptures, seek out God's voice individually, and go to trusted advisors. This theme does not *discourage* people from seeking the encouragement or advice of friends, but instead advises against relying wholly on those human voices during trials and hardships. Advice from friends can be valuable, but it should never replace God's guidance.

5. Dangers of Religious Presumption

Job's friends spoke confidently on God's behalf, yet they did not truly understand Him. They applied rigid theology with little compassion or discernment, assuming their perspective was complete. The danger here is clear: when we speak for God without first seeking His wisdom and interpretation, we risk misrepresenting Him. *Even with good intentions, misguided theology can cause real harm.* This is why knowing Scripture for ourselves is essential—especially when speaking into another person's hardship.

6. Restoration and Redemption

God can redeem loss, but not always in the way we expect. God redeems Job's loss with a double portion of what he had lost, though the pain of his past isn't erased. Restoration doesn't erase the journey; it's part of the purpose. If we are to forget those moments of pain and difficulty, the growth and transformation would also be forgotten and wasted.

7. Forgive and Bless Others

Before restoring Job, God instructs him to intercede for the very friends who wronged him, highlighting that, *even in pain, the righteous are called to forgive and intercede even those who have wronged them* (Job 42:8). Despite being accused, wronged, slandered, humiliated, and judged harshly by his friends, God doesn't leave those wounds of Job's heart unaddressed. Forgiveness was necessary for Job's transformation to be complete. When he forgave and blessed, this showed his full, complete heart-transformation. Job's story teaches that – in a world of brokenness and unanswered questions – enduring faith, honest lament, and deep reverence for God form the path to true wisdom.

Now What?

There's so much to say about the Book of Job and how it applies to life today – though I'll admit, I didn't see it until adulthood, after walking through my own hardships and studying Job for myself. I hope you can see that the book isn't something to be feared but rather to be treasured as a valuable resource for your heart during a season of painful growth and fire-filled transformation.

As I've walked through my own wilderness seasons and refining fires, I've often wished for a book like this. Honestly, even as I've been writing these chapters, I've felt the weight of my journey's hardships. Whether this trial is an attack from the enemy or God's hand of maturing, I can almost hear Him saying, "You've learned these truths – now live them, even as you write them." Either way, these revelations have been just as encouraging to me in this season as I pray they will be for you.

Before we move on, here's a reminder of the three self-reflection and application steps you'll find at the end of each chapter. These are designed to help you walk out what you've learned.

1. **Pause on the Path**: A short devotional thought that recaps the chapter's key idea and brings it to *your* heart's level.

2. **Putting It Into Practice**: Concrete, practical next steps you can take to live out what you've studied, reflected on, and learned.

3. **Prayer for the Journey**: A short, Christ-centered prayer to help you offer the lesson back to God and to apply it to your life from a surrendered heart.

Now that you know what to expect, let's dive into how we can take these challenging stories and apply them to your life.

Pause on the Path

Job's journey reminds us that faith is not refined in comfort but in the fire. Like Job, you may begin in a season of blessing and doing all of the right things! Then, in a sudden turn of events, you find yourself being thrust without warning into profound loss, grief, and questions. Job's Hero's Journey was not about escaping pain but discovering that *God's presence is greater than answers*, and *His purposes are bigger than what Job could see*.

The same can be applied to you and me. His presence really is worth more than any answers. His purposes are bigger than anything we can think or imagine. Even though the pain and grief may feel like more than you can bear, God is still greater, still faithful, still living, and with you through it all. In the end, Job encountered God more deeply, and his faith emerged refined like gold. God will always restore that which has been lost, stolen, or broken. It's important to remember that His restoration doesn't mean He will restore things in the way *we desire* or that the pain will magically dissipate. However, God will always use the pain to fulfill His purposes in your life.

Putting It into Practice

Write: Journal about one way God has revealed Himself to you during a season of hardship - either in a current or past season. Remind yourself of all that God has taught you or encouraged you with. What emotions did you feel (or are currently feeling)? What fears did you face in the journey? What truths have you learned about God in the journey?

Pray: Instead of asking only for answers, pray for a deeper awareness of God's nearness. Remember, *God's presence is greater than answers*, and *His purposes are bigger than what you can see*. Spend some time really asking for the Lord to meet you and to experience His presence. Try to avoid asking for answers, and focus instead on seeking His face and His presence.

Act: This week, choose one area of suffering or confusion in your life and consciously entrust it to God's sovereignty. Like Job, refuse to curse God in your trial but instead reaffirm His lordship over your life. Take one step — write a note of encouragement to someone else in hardship, pray with them, or share your testimony of God's sustaining grace.

Each morning, begin with Job's declaration: *"The LORD gave, and the LORD has taken away; blessed be the name of the LORD"* (Job 1:21). Sing or listen to a song of surrender and praise — even if you don't feel like it — as a defiant act of trust in God's goodness.

Reach out to someone in a "storm season" and be the kind of friend Job needed — present, prayerful, and compassionate. Resist the urge to explain or fix their pain. Instead, gently point them to Christ, who is *"a man of sorrows and acquainted with grief"* (Isaiah 53:3).

Prayer for the Journey

Father, I confess that I do not always understand Your ways, but I trust Your heart. I repent for any anger towards you in this season. Please soften my heart to that of Job's heart position. When trials come and affliction hits hard, help me to fall on my face in worship before you. Like Job, I choose to bless Your name in both giving and taking away. You are the Divine Author and know more than I could ever wrap my mind around. Your ways are higher than my ways. Help me never forget that. Refine my faith through trials, and let my life declare that my Redeemer lives. I want to be Your instrument for Your purposes. I surrender my heart to you even in the midst of the pain, hardship, and calamity. I am Yours. In Jesus' name, Amen.

CHAPTER 5

Abraham: Walking by Faith When the Map Is Blank

Abraham's story begins when God spoke directly to him: "Leave what you know, walk into what I will show, and I will make you into a great nation." The promise was clear and specific! However, the path was not. What followed was twenty-five years of trusting, waiting, and learning to maintain faith amidst the uncertainty. Something important to note about Abraham was that his faith did not grow in a straight line. His faith grew in the Potter's kiln—through famine, family tensions, missteps with Hagar, and long stretches where nothing seemed to change. Yet through the waiting, God was not absent; He was working and forming.

The God Who Forms in the Waiting

If you've ever clung to a word from the Lord while the timeline stretched far beyond what you imagined, you're in good company! I have too. Some promises in my own life remain unfulfilled. In my own season of waiting, the Potter has pressed and reshaped me—especially in the area of pride. Those seasons remind me that God never wastes our wilderness; He uses it to deepen our trust in Him, to purify our hearts' motives, and to prepare us for the weight of what He intends to give.

Abraham wasn't spiritually "ready" or mature enough on day one—and neither are we! But here's the beauty of the waiting season: God, who calls us when we aren't yet ready, cultivates us until we are. He sees our weaknesses *and* our potential. He meets us in our mess. This truth touches my heart deeply. Even in my own hardship, God met me at my lowest moments. He has not abandoned you, either. He sees you in your mess, loves you, and calls you higher. If you surrender your journey to the Master Storywriter, He can weave your brokenness into a masterful story of growth, transformation, and new life. As the Divine Potter, He patiently molds and forms in us the kind of faith that can hold a miracle. Abraham's life is a testament to this truth!

From Abram to Abraham: Faith Grown in Waiting

Abraham, initially named Abram, is introduced in the book of Genesis as "a man from Ur of the Chaldeans," an ancient Mesopotamian city. Scripture gives us only a glimpse of Abram's backstory in Genesis 11:26-32. We are told of his family lineage, marriage to Sarai (later Sarah), and his father Terah's partial journey toward Canaan before settling in Haran. And that's all we are told. In this initial introduction to Abram, we see a man who still seems to live in the shadow of his father. However, Abraham's life took a pivotal turn in Genesis 12 when God called him to leave his homeland and his family and travel to a land that He would show him:

> *"Now the LORD said to Abram, 'Go from your country and your kindred and your father's house to the land that I will show you. And I will make of you a great nation, and I will bless you and make your name great, so that you will be a blessing. I will bless those who bless you, and him who dishonors you I will curse, and in you all the families of the earth shall be blessed.' So Abram went, as the LORD had told him…" (Genesis 12:1-4a).*

In this call, God made a profound promise: to make Abram into a great nation, to bless him, and to make his name great. In faith, Abraham obeyed, embarking on a journey that would define not only his life but also the course of Biblical and world history. It was his immense faith in the promise of the Lord that led him to be called "the father of our faith." Yet Abraham's path was not without wilderness seasons and testing. He wasn't perfect and made his fair share of mistakes – one of which, most notably, led to the human-crafted arrangement with Hagar and the birth of a son, Ishmael. During a famine, when he traveled to Egypt, he even misrepresented himself as Sarah's brother. This happened TWICE! However, the Lord was still faithful to His servant Abram. The Lord even changed his name from Abram to Abraham, which means "father of many" (Genesis 17), and Sarai to Sarah, meaning "princess."

As Abraham traveled through Canaan, God repeatedly affirmed His promises, deepening his faith. Despite being childless and advanced in age, Abraham was told that his descendants would be as numerous as the stars. Against all odds, and after twenty-five years of waiting, Sarah gave birth to Isaac. The wait is *central* to Abraham's story – twenty-five years of trusting God's word without seeing its fulfillment. *Twenty-five years*. This is an important thing I really came to appreciate about Abraham, the father of our faith: the wait! He waited and waited and believed and believed. In fact, Paul later states this about Abraham's faithfulness to the Lord:

> *"In hope he believed against hope, that he should become the father of many nations, as he had been told, 'So shall your offspring be.' He did not weaken in faith when he considered his own body, which was as good as dead (since he was about a hundred years old), or when he considered the barrenness of Sarah's womb.* **No unbelief made him waver concerning the promise of God, but he grew strong in his faith as he gave glory to God, fully convinced that God was able to do what he had promised**" *(Romans 4:18-21).*

"No unbelief made him waver."

"Fully convinced that God was able to do what he had promised."

Despite Abraham's mistakes and sins, God reaffirmed and responded to Abraham's faithfulness throughout the twenty-five years of waiting. Abraham's unwavering faith reached its pinnacle when God asked him to sacrifice Isaac (see Genesis 22:1-19). After decades of trust, Abraham obeyed without hesitation and trusted God even in this unthinkable command. At the last moment, God stopped Abraham and provided a ram for the offering. This act of obedience from Abraham confirmed Abraham's complete trust in the Lord.

Like Job, Abraham's long season of waiting is another striking example of the Lord's masterful storytelling through His divine plotline: The Hero's Journey. We see the impact of God's vision of potential within the lives of ordinary people. God looked into the life of Abram, a simple man living in the shadow of his father, and saw all that he could be. Yet God knew Abram would need years of testing, trial, and growth before becoming the man who would not even withhold his son from the Giver of life. In His infinite wisdom, God knew exactly how to grow him into the man who would become the father of a nation and of our faith. The Hero's Journey reveals this transformation as the Potter's hands mold Abram into Abraham, the father of our faith. To see a complete outline of Abraham's Hero's Journey, see Appendix 2.

Faith That Does Not Waver

God commends Abraham's faithfulness in the great Hall of Faith in Hebrews 11 when the author of Hebrews says, *"[Abraham] considered that God was able even to raise him from the dead..."* (Hebrews 11:19). Abraham had developed such a profound theology of absolute faith in his twenty-five years of waiting for the promise that he sincerely believed that, when God asked for his only son as a sacrifice, it meant God intended to raise Isaac from the dead. Abraham's faith was true and complete, holding back nothing from the Lord.

If his life could be summed up in one verse, it would be found in Romans 4:20: *"No unbelief made him waver concerning the promise of God, but he grew strong in his faith as he gave glory to God, fully convinced that God was able to do what he had promised"* (Romans 4:20-21). What a tremendous statement of God's opinion of this man that perfectly explains the life of faith Abraham lived - flaws, sins, victories, and all! After walking my own seasons of waiting, my prayer is that the Lord might one day say the same of me. Abraham's story shows that the waiting season is not wasted – it is where faith deepens and trust becomes unshakable.

Key Themes from the Journey of Abraham

Seen through the lens of The Hero's Journey, Abraham is a spiritual pioneer who leaves behind the familiar to follow God's divine calling. He faces doubts, trials, and near-tragedies, yet he emerges transformed, a new creation having endured the Potter's wheel and the fires of His kiln. His story is not one of conquest or physical might, but of trust, obedience, and enduring legacy—a hero not by worldly standards, but by divine purpose.

1. Faith in God's Promises

Called the father of faith, Abraham trusted God's word when belief seemed impossible. God promised descendants as numerous as the stars when Abraham was old and Sarah had been barren for decades. His faith reached its peak when God asked him to sacrifice Isaac, the son of promise. Even then, Abraham trusted that God would raise Isaac from the dead if necessary (Hebrews 11:17–19). His life testified to a faith anchored not in visible results but in the unshakable character of God.

2. Obedience and Surrender

Abraham responded to God's initial call with bold obedience, leaving his home and family for an unknown land simply because God said to go (Genesis 12:1–4). He didn't have the whole picture, yet he moved forward in faith. This pattern of surrender marked his life. Whether choosing peace with Lot by giving him the better land, accepting circumcision as a covenant sign, or preparing to offer his son on the altar, Abraham consistently laid down his own understanding in favor of trusting God's leadership. His obedience wasn't perfect, but it grew deeper with every step, showing that surrender to God often happens one act of trust at a time.

3. Covenant Relationship

God's covenant with Abraham established a defining moment not only in Abraham's life, but in the overarching narrative of Scripture. God promised him land, descendants, and blessing, and confirmed it through a formal covenant ceremony (Genesis 15). This relationship was not built on Abraham's merit or performance, but on God's sovereign grace and unwavering faithfulness. God bound Himself to Abraham and his offspring, initiating a lasting relationship that revealed His desire to dwell with and bless humanity. Abraham's story became a foundation of Israel's national identity, showing that belonging to God was rooted in promise, not human perfection.

4. Testing and Refinement

Abraham's journey with God was far from easy. He endured famines, family conflicts, and long periods of silence from God. At times, he failed—such as when he lied about Sarah being his sister or tried to fulfill God's promise through Hagar—but these trials and setbacks didn't disqualify him. Instead, they became the means through which God refined his character and grew his faith. Every challenge served a greater purpose in deepening Abraham's dependence on the Lord. Over time, he learned to trust God's timing and goodness more fully. His life demonstrated that testing is not punishment, but preparation for a deeper partnership with God.

5. Blessing for the Nations

Abraham's life was never just about him. From the beginning, God made it clear that Abraham would be a channel of blessing to others: *"Through you all the families of the earth shall be blessed"* (Genesis 12:3). This promise found ultimate fulfillment in Jesus Christ, a descendant of Abraham, through whom salvation would come to the world (Galatians 3:8, 16). Abraham's story showed that God's purposes are global, timeless, and redemptive, reaching far beyond individual blessings to bring healing and hope to the nations. He lived not just as a recipient of God's favor, but as a vessel through which God carried out His redemptive plan.

Pause on the Path

Abraham's story reminds us that God's promises often require leaving what's familiar before seeing what's next. Faith rarely comes with a roadmap—it comes with a word. Like Abraham, we are often called to *go* without knowing *where we are going.* His journey teaches us that obedience opens the door to revelation, and waiting refines our trust. Through famine, failure, and long years of silence, Abraham learned that God's covenant doesn't depend on perfect faith, but on a faithful God. His story points to Christ—the ultimate promised Son—through whom all nations are blessed.

Putting It into Practice

Write: In your journal, reflect on a time when God asked you to take a step of faith without giving you all the details. How did you respond? Journal about what He revealed to you in the process.

Pray: Ask God to give you Abraham's courage to obey even when the path feels unclear. Pray for the grace to release control and believe that His promises will stand—even when the timeline feels impossible.

Act: Take one small step of obedience this week toward something God has already spoken to you about. It may be starting, surrendering, or staying—whatever it is, do it in faith.

Worship: Meditate on Romans 4:20–21: *"No unbelief made him waver concerning the promise of God, but he grew strong in his faith… fully convinced that God was able to do what he had promised."* Thank God for the promises He has already fulfilled, and praise Him for those still unfolding.

Prayer for the Journey

Lord, I want to follow You like Abraham did—with faith that moves even when I don't understand the path ahead. Strengthen my heart to obey without seeing the full picture. Remind me that Your promises never fail and that waiting is not wasted. Teach me to trust You in the silence, knowing You are forming in me the faith that can hold the miracle. I surrender my timeline to You. Let my obedience bring glory to Your name. In Jesus' name, Amen.

CHAPTER 6
Joseph: From Dreams to Detours

Joseph's story begins with *dreams*—glimpses of a future still too bright for where he was emotionally and spiritually in his present. Unbeknownst to Joseph, between the dream and the destiny lay twenty-two years of heartwrenching detours: betrayal, slavery, false accusation, prison, and the ache of being forgotten and abandoned. Although he was called to leadership and greatness, God still saw the rough edges that needed to be refined and pruned off of Joseph. In every low place he encountered, God was preparing him for a *very* high calling, training his character to match the influence he would one day hold.

The Refining in the Waiting

If your life has taken a turn that seems to contradict what God promised, you're not alone. I've known those turns all too well (and in some harrowing ways). In my own waiting, the Potter has crushed and remade places in my heart that I simply didn't expect. Through his molding and refining, He again and again reminded me that He is *ever*-present, not only in the fulfillment of promise but also in the formation. Joseph discovered the same truth: God's faithfulness is always active and working on our behalf. *His faithfulness is active even in the darkest seasons, shaping us for the day the light will break through!*

Like Abraham, Joseph wasn't ready when God first called him. He was roughly seventeen when he first had the dream. He was not prepared to hold the position of authority and leadership God had called him to—and God knew it. The Lord meets us where we are, yes! And He calls us even higher! However, to get us to that higher place, He teaches us integrity in *hidden* places. He infuses us with humility through unjust seasons. Your job is to surrender your story to the Master Storywriter and watch Him redeem the detours. In His hands, even the pit and the prison become chapters of purpose—woven into a testimony of transformation and new life.

Joseph's story has become one of my favorite places to turn to when I'm feeling discouraged in my waiting season and testing. This man went from the favored son of an older father to the pits of despair to complete power and authority. God called him as a young man, long before he was ready for the role He had in mind.

From the Pit to the Palace

Joseph was the eleventh son of Jacob and the firstborn of Rachel, Jacob's favorite wife. From a young age, Joseph stood out to his father and was favored above his ten older brothers. Jacob showed this favoritism by gifting him a richly ornamented coat — often referred to as the "coat of many colors." In this time period, colored linen would be much more costly than plain fabrics. God also gave Joseph two prophetic dreams of immense favor and destiny. But, in youthful naivety (or pride), Joseph shared them with his family, which only fueled the bitterness and envy within his brothers.

One day, Jacob sent Joseph to check on his brothers in the fields. Seeing him approach, they plotted against him—at first intending to kill him, but instead throwing him into a dry cistern and later selling him to Ishmaelite traders bound for Egypt. To conceal their sinister deed, they dipped Joseph's robe in a goat's blood and presented it to Jacob, who believed a wild animal had killed his beloved son.

In Egypt, Joseph was sold as a slave to Potiphar, a high-ranking official under Pharaoh. Joseph quickly gained his master's trust and was made overseer of Potiphar's household. When Potiphar's wife tried to seduce Joseph and he refused, she falsely accused him of assault. As a result, Joseph was thrown into prison—seemingly abandoned, yet still under God's watchful care.

Even in prison, Joseph found favor. The prison warden entrusted him with responsibilities, and he eventually met two of Pharaoh's officials, the cupbearer and the baker, who had been thrown in prison as well. While in prison, these two men dreamt disturbing dreams. Joseph interpreted their dreams accurately. The cupbearer was restored, and the baker was executed—just as Joseph had said. Joseph asked the cupbearer to remember him once restored, but the man forgot. Joseph remained in prison for two more years. Throughout all of this waiting and imprisonment, God was working in Joseph's heart to prepare him to be the man God needed him to be when Joseph was called into his position of power and leadership.

Then, Pharaoh himself had troubling dreams: seven healthy cows being devoured by seven scrawny ones, and seven full ears of grain being consumed by seven thin ones. None of his advisors could interpret them! These dreams left everyone feeling perplexed, and tormented the Pharaoh. Because of the intensity of these dreams, the cupbearer remembered Joseph and told Pharaoh about his dream interpretation. The Pharaoh summoned Joseph from prison to the palace. Joseph, in a tremendous act of divine, God-given wisdom, interprets the dream for Pharaoh and gives specific directions for implementing the interpretation. And Joseph gave God the credit for his ability! He interpreted the dreams as this: seven years of abundance would be followed by seven years of severe famine. Impressed, Pharaoh appointed Joseph as second-in-command over all Egypt, tasking him with overseeing food storage during the plentiful years.

After seven years of plenty, the famine struck, but Egypt was prepared. Approximately two years in, Joseph's brothers finally came to Egypt to buy grain. When his brothers finally arrived, they no longer recognized him, for many years had passed. Joseph, however, recognized them! Rather than revealing himself immediately, he tested their hearts. He accused them of being spies, imprisoned Simeon, and demanded Benjamin's presence. They returned home discouraged.

Months went by, and the food Jacob's family had purchased in Egypt had run out. Jacob directed his nine remaining sons to return (remember, Simeon was still imprisoned in Egypt) for more food. This time, they brought Benjamin with them as Joseph demanded. When they returned, Joseph hosted them for a meal. To test their hearts, he planted a silver cup in Benjamin's sack and then accused him of theft. This led to a moment of truth: Judah, once the ringleader in Joseph's betrayal, now offered to take Benjamin's place as a slave. This selfless act from Judah showed the repentance and transformation within Judah's heart and was a reflection of the change within the other brothers as well. Overcome with emotion, Joseph revealed his identity, weeping so loudly it was heard throughout Pharaoh's house.

What God Meant for Good

Rather than seeking revenge, Joseph comforted his brothers: *"You meant evil against me, but God meant it for good, to save many lives"* (Genesis 50:20). This massive statement from Joseph truly demonstrated the immense transformation that took place within his heart. He understood how God used his prison season to elevate him spiritually, enabling him to occupy the highest physical position of power in Pharaoh's court.

Joseph assured his brothers of his forgiveness, released Simeon from prison, and invited the entire family, including his aged father Jacob, to live in Egypt under his protection. Jacob was overjoyed to see his son alive and spent his final years in Egypt. Before his death, Jacob ended up blessing Joseph's two sons, Ephraim and Manasseh, as his own sons!

Whereas Abraham endured a tremendous season of *waiting*, Joseph survived a long season of *betrayal, slavery, and prison*. This was the refining process God, in His infinite wisdom, knew was needed to prepare him for the power and authority he would one day carry. Joseph's season of calamity is another Biblical example that reflects The Hero's Journey step by step! Read each step in detail found in Appendix 3 at the back of the book.

Throughout his story, we clearly see how God used pain, hardship, trials, imprisonment, and betrayal to grow Joseph into the man God needed him to be. When Joseph received the Lord's prophetic dreams, he was *not ready* to assume that position of power. This is evident in his somewhat ignorant blabbing about the dreams. Either he was clueless about his brothers' feelings towards him for being the favored son, which seems unlikely, or he simply didn't care that they were already jealous and bitter towards him and told them anyway! Either way, there were some serious heart issues that God needed to work out of Joseph before He could place

Joseph on the throne of Egypt. His journey was exactly what God *knew* Joseph required to fulfill his destiny. Even Joseph admits his knowledge of this to his brothers when he said to them, *"God sent me ahead of you to preserve for you a remnant on earth and to save your lives by a great deliverance. 8 So then, it was not you who sent me here, but God. He made me father to Pharaoh, lord of his entire household and ruler of all Egypt"* (Genesis 45:7-8). By the end of his journey, when the promise given to him as a much younger man was finally fulfilled, Joseph confessed the hand of the Lord on his entire journey. He admits that this was precisely what he needed to walk through for God's will to be done.

This perspective is what I hope you, dear reader, will also gain: to view your journey through the lens of God's hand shaping you. There is such hope in the midst of every trial and season of calamity – even when we can't see it at the moment. As James writes: *"Count it all joy, my brothers, when you meet trials of various kinds, for you know that the testing of your faith produces steadfastness. And let steadfastness have its full effect, that you may be perfect and complete, lacking in nothing"* (James 1:2–4). When we start to see our journey as Joseph did, we can truly begin to view the testing with joy and walk through it with steadfastness, so that we may be made *perfect and complete, lacking in nothing!*

Key Themes from the Life of Joseph

Joseph's journey is one of betrayal, perseverance, divine favor, and redemption. His faith and integrity, even in suffering, lead him to fulfill a divine purpose, saving nations and reconciling his broken family.

1. Divine Providence

Divine Providence is the conviction that God is actively at work, even when His hand isn't immediately visible. Joseph's life demonstrated this truth vividly. Though he was sold into slavery by jealous brothers, falsely accused by Potiphar's wife, and forgotten in prison, none of these injustices thwarted God's plan. Instead, they became essential steps toward his appointment as second-in-command of Egypt. Through these hardships, God orchestrated events to place Joseph in a position to preserve not only the Egyptian nation but also the future of Israel. Joseph himself acknowledges this truth in Genesis 45:5–8 and 50:20, recognizing that it was ultimately God—not his brothers—who sent him to Egypt for a redemptive purpose. His story reassures believers that, even when life feels derailed, God's purpose is never defeated.

2. Faithfulness in Suffering

Throughout years of adversity, Joseph remained faithful. He served with integrity in Potiphar's house, resisted temptation, and conducted himself with humility in prison. Despite being forgotten and falsely accused, he didn't become bitter or give up. He honored God quietly through his actions, trusting that the Lord had not abandoned him. God's presence was with him even behind bars (Genesis 39:21), and Joseph's consistent character earned him favor wherever he went. His long season of waiting refined him and prepared him for the responsibilities he would later carry.

3. Forgiveness and Reconciliation

When Joseph finally stood before the brothers who had sold him into slavery, he chose forgiveness over revenge. After testing their hearts, he revealed his identity with compassion, embraced them, and extended forgiveness. His forgiveness led to reconciliation not only with his brothers but also within the fractured family of Israel. By refusing to let bitterness take root, Joseph restored what had once been broken. His actions reflected the heart of God and laid the foundation for family healing (Genesis 45:1–15).

4. Wisdom and Stewardship

Joseph didn't use his God-given abilities for personal gain. When Pharaoh called on him to interpret dreams, Joseph gave all credit to God (Genesis 41:16) and used that wisdom to propose a plan that saved Egypt from famine. As a steward of great responsibility, he managed resources with excellence, compassion, wisdom, and foresight. His leadership saved many lives and stabilized the region during the famine crisis. Joseph proved that wisdom is not just in understanding truth, but in applying it selflessly for the benefit of others.

5. God's sovereignty over human actions

Joseph's life ultimately revealed that God's purposes override every human decision. What his brothers intended for harm, God used to bring life and restoration. Though Joseph endured great injustice, his life testified to the truth that nothing could derail God's purposes. He saw that every betrayal and hardship had been part of a much bigger plan. In the end, Joseph declared with confidence, *"You meant evil against me, but God meant it for good"* (Genesis 50:20). His life demonstrated that God could redeem any situation and bring good from what was intended for harm.

Pause on the Path

Joseph's journey reminds us that God's favor doesn't mean exemption from suffering. Sometimes His greatest work takes place in the pit, the prison, or the waiting room. From betrayal to redemption, Joseph's story proves that what others mean for harm, God can use for good—not only for our growth but for the saving of many lives. The same hand that allowed the pain is the one that will weave it into purpose. Your waiting is not punishment—it's preparation.

Putting It into Practice

Write: Recall a past hardship where, in hindsight, you can now see God's redemptive hand. How did He use it to shape your heart or redirect your path? Write about it as a testimony of His faithfulness.

Pray: Ask for Joseph's endurance—to keep trusting God's unseen work in the detours. Invite Him to transform bitterness into blessing and confusion into clarity.

Act: Identify one place in your life where forgiveness is still needed. Take one tangible step toward release: pray for that person, write a letter you may never send, or choose to bless them privately.

Encourage: Think of someone who feels stuck in a "pit" or "prison" season. Reach out and share how God met you in your own waiting. Remind them that hidden seasons can still be holy seasons.

Declare: Meditate on Genesis 50:20: *"You meant evil against me, but God meant it for good."* Use it as a declaration over your own life.

Prayer for the Journey

Father, thank You for being present even in the detours. When I feel forgotten, remind me that You are still working behind the scenes. Shape my heart like Joseph's—steadfast, humble, and quick to forgive. Help me to trust Your timing, to see purpose in the pain, and to believe that You are using my story for Your glory. Teach me to rest in Your redemption, even when I cannot yet see the end. In Jesus' name, Amen.

CHAPTER 7

Moses: When the Wilderness Becomes Holy Ground

Abraham waited 25 years for his promise. Joseph's wait stretched 17–22 years. Job endured tremendous trials, too, but we are not told how long they lasted. Of the lives in the Bible, however, no one's wait was longer than Moses' wait—most of his life was marked by delay and preparation. His story unfolds in three 40-year seasons.

Although the first 40 years of his life were spent in Pharaoh's palace, God knew Moses needed the wilderness season to shape his heart. After fleeing Egypt in fear for his life, Moses spent 40 years hiding in the wilderness as a shepherd, hidden from power but not from God's refining hand. After being molded in the wilderness, God called Moses back to Egypt to be the vessel of God's power and messenger to the people of Israel. From his return to Egypt, Moses spent another 40 years leading the people of Israel.

Moses endured decades of personal renewal and wilderness wandering. This may come across as unfair or intimidating, but through his waiting period, this evident truth emerges: he encountered the presence and glory of the Living God in a way no other man has! The men and women of the Bible who waited and endured the most complex trials received the *greatest* rewards from God Almighty. God does not just dole out His promises, anointing, power, and authority to just anyone. He only entrusts these things to those who have walked through the crushing of the Potter's wheel and the fire of His kiln. As Bob Sorge says, "The greater the wait, the greater the work.... No one else in the Bible (apart from Jesus) knew the glory of God like Moses did" (Sorge, 1996). And Moses' post-wait encounters prove it: the burning bush, the ten plagues, the parting of the Red Sea, water from the rock, manna and quail from heaven, and many more miracles. He even encountered the actual presence of God on Mt. Sinai, received the Law from God, and spent so much time in the Lord's presence that his face literally GLOWED with radiation from the Lord's presence! And, to top it all off, he actually got to SEE God physically, even if it was just His backside as He walked away from Moses (to keep Moses from dying). These miracles and divine moments flowed from decades of unseen, often painful preparation—showing that the wait was not wasted.

The Wilderness and the Refiner's Fire

This truth can feel intimidating: "Ummm, God, I don't really WANT to wait 40 years for this problem to be resolved!" I know I don't! My daughter—the child of my promise—would be 46 by then! Yikes. Yet Moses' story reminds us that long seasons of waiting and molding are not wasted. Our God does miraculous things with His saints. And He does even greater with those who are willing to pray, "Lord, I trust you in the process. Mold me. Use me. I am yours!" This is when true transformation happens. And this isn't just some "Christianese" rule I am trying to convince you of. This is straight from Scripture:

> **Job 23:10** *"But He knows the way that I take; when He has tried me, I shall come out as gold."*

> **Psalm 66:10-12** *"For You, God, tested us; you refined us like silver. You brought us into prison and laid burdens on our backs. You let people ride over our heads; we went through fire and water, but You brought us to a place of abundance."*

Proverbs 17:3 *"The crucible is for silver, and the furnace is for gold, and the LORD tests hearts."*

Malachi 3:3 *"He will sit as a refiner and purifier of silver, and He will purify the sons of Levi and refine them like gold and silver, and they will bring offerings in righteousness to the LORD."*

1 Peter 1:6 *"In this you rejoice, though now for a little while, if necessary, you have been grieved by various trials. These have come so that the proven genuineness of your faith—of greater worth than gold, which perishes even though refined by fire—may result in praise, glory, and honor when Jesus Christ is revealed."*

These verses reveal how God works on the hearts of His beloved—through the refining fire of His furnace. Intimidating? Yes. However, I would encourage you in this: of all that this world has to offer, is not God Himself, His divine revelation, presence, and anointing worth any cost? Absolutely.

Moses spent 40 years of his life in the wilderness *as a shepherd*. It's important to note here that Egyptians thought shepherding was the lowest of positions. Joseph explained this to his family in Genesis 46 before they settled in Goshen: *"When Pharaoh calls you in and asks, 'What is your occupation?' you should answer, 'Your servants have tended livestock from our boyhood on, just as our fathers did.' Then you will be allowed to settle in the region of Goshen, for **all shepherds are an abomination to the Egyptians"*** (Genesis 46: 34). The Hebrew word used there for *abomination* is the word *"toeba" (toe-ay-vaw)*. According to the Blue Letter Bible interlinear concordance, *toeba* in Hebrew means "something disgusting (morally), an abhorrence... abominable" (BLB). Other Bible translations use these words to describe "toeba": despicable, loathsome, detestable, and repulsive.

As a prince of Egypt raised in Pharaoh's palace, Moses would have shared this cultural disdain for shepherds: they are despicable, loathsome, detestable, and repulsive. After he fled Egypt, God placed him in the very role he'd been raised to see as disgusting. Think of the absolute grossest job you can think of. And now, imagine God placing you to work for 40 years in *that exact job*. For Moses, this was a profoundly humbling process, stripping away palace pride and preparing him for servant leadership.

    I imagine him struggling with the thoughts of "God, you rescued me from Pharaoh as an infant, just to bring me here? As a shepherd?" God used the palace, yes, to save and preserve Moses for His purposes, but now God needed to work the palace *out* of Moses. What better way than to place him in the exact position he was raised to believe was disgusting? I can't speak for you, but for me, this understanding of Moses' 40 years in the wilderness really opened my eyes to the work God had to do in Moses' heart.

    The life of Moses, recorded in Exodus, Leviticus, Numbers, and Deuteronomy, offers another strong testimony to the pen of our Almighty Storycreator-God. His story aligns seamlessly with The Hero's Journey structure. I have laid it out in detail in Appendix 4 at the back of the book. Throughout Moses' life, we see numerous cycles of The Hero's Journey, both large and small, while his life fits within a grand-scale Hero's Journey. At the same time, many individual episodes — such as the burning bush, the plagues, or the wilderness wanderings — form smaller journeys that build into the greater whole. Check Appendix 4 for all the details.

Wilderness Survival Tools

When reading about Moses' wilderness season, it's normal to feel intimidated. However, the wilderness season is where God can do His greatest molding in your heart for ultimate growth. We ALL have areas in our hearts and lives that need pruning and refining, but this does not need to scare us! Remember, Paul tells us in Romans that *"The Spirit helps us in our weakness.... the Spirit intercedes for the saints according to the will of God. And we know that for those who love God all things work together for good, for those who are called according to his purpose"* (Romans 8:26-28). This is one of the greatest verses we could quote in this book, as it holds so much hope for anyone walking through a season of hardship. Whether you are in a season of calamity like Job, waiting like Abraham, imprisonment like Joseph, or wilderness like Moses, the Lord promises two crucial survival tools in this verse in Romans.

    The first tool here is this: knowing that the Holy Spirit Himself is in the Throneroom of Heaven, *praying specifically for **us**.* God does not abandon us to stumble through the trials. No! God, in his infinite goodness and faithfulness, has sent us the Helper, the Holy Spirit, to "help us in our weakness," to intercede (or fervently pray) for us, and to orchestrate all the circumstances surrounding us for **our good!** This is a "praise the Lord" moment if I ever heard one! We are not alone in this journey! We have the Holy Spirit as a personal friend and intercessor in our times of calamity, waiting, imprisonment, or wandering.

The second tool in this verse is the knowledge that *God will always use ALL THINGS for our good.* That means the good, the bad, and the ugly; God will use it for your good. Now, **this doesn't permit us to live in sin.** We can't just claim "Oh, God's going to use this for my good!" while deliberately living in rebellion. That is an abuse of God's grace. I know this from personal experience. James very clearly addresses this behavior and mindset when he says, *"Therefore, put away all filthiness and rampant wickedness and receive with meekness the implanted word, which can save your souls. But be doers of the word, and not hearers only, deceiving yourselves."* And later, James also says, *"Show me your faith apart from your works, and I will show you my faith by my works"* (James 1:21–22 and 2:18). A genuine relationship with God moves us *away* from sin and *toward* obedience. This movement towards God, as James says, is seen by our works—not in a stuffy, religious way, but as a relationship demonstrated.

The same can be said of marriage. When I married my husband, my actions changed. I no longer flirted or sought other relationships, because my devotion belonged to him. The same is true of our walk with Jesus: when we love Him, our lives reflect it..

My Own Wilderness Season

This second tool brings me much comfort, because I once lived in a way that abused God's grace. Earlier, I shared how pride marked much of my youth, though I didn't recognize it at the time. I was a three-sport athlete, played multiple instruments, volunteered at church, held a job, earned straight A's, graduated at the top of my class, and received a prestigious scholarship available in the state of Oregon. Life looked perfect. In college, the same pattern continued: good grades, scholarships, and success in athletics. I even remember a cousin telling me I was the example of "what happens when you do everything right." And I believed it, and my pride swelled. That pride was also the beginning of my downfall (Remember Proverbs 16:18? *"Pride goes before destruction…"*).

As temptations came—lying, drinking, partying, fornication—I stepped into them without fear of God. Pride dulled my conscience. I justified myself by thinking my "good works" outweighed my sin. I even twisted grace into an excuse, telling myself, "God's grace is sufficient for me." The truth? I thought I was above God's holiness, but correction came.

Like Moses, God led me into my wilderness. There were some serious things that God needed to prune, crush, refine, and mold in me *and out of me*. My prideful choices and spiritual blindness led me into a toxic, unsafe marriage. I remember, even before the wedding, hearing a pounding voice in my spirit—now I know it was the Holy Spirit—urging me not to walk down that aisle. But I cared more about appearances than obedience. Pride won again, and I entered a marriage that quickly became destructive, toxic, and dangerous, and things only got worse and worse for me as the months turned into years. I felt myself becoming a shell of who I used to be.

It was in that season, through the pain of marriage and then divorce, that God tore down my pride. He showed me I could not live outside His will. After nearly three years, He gave me a vision and a promise that shook me. Terrified and humiliated, I finally left. And though I felt broken, insecure, and alone, I had no choice but to cling to Him. On the Potter's wheel, God crushed my pride and built in me faith and dependence.

Looking back at that season, I can see Romans 8:26-28 at work in my life. The Holy Spirit was there with me, in fear and behind closed doors, when no one else was there. The Holy Spirit was praying for me, interceding for me before the Throne of Heaven. And indeed, the Lord *did* work all of that out for my good. Although broken-hearted and humiliated, God broke me of my pride, my sinful lifestyles, and the desire for human approval. He brought me to my knees in complete surrender to Him. I was crushed, molded, refined, and placed in the fire of affliction, as the book of Isaiah says, *"Behold, I have refined you, but not as silver; I have tried you in the furnace of affliction"* (Isaiah 48:10). The Lord brought me into the wilderness season. Though I felt abandoned, God was my closest companion, and that's exactly where He wanted me—surrendered and finally in His hands. That's when the refining could take place.

Maybe you're like me (and like Moses), and you need some things worked out of your life. If you have found yourself in a place where God seems to be your only solace, be encouraged: God is working a great thing in you! Don't lose heart! In time, you will be able to stand where I stand, looking *back* at the wilderness season with a fresh understanding of all that God has done in your heart.

Key Themes from the Life of Moses

The life of Moses is rich with enduring themes that span growth, transformation, courage, leadership, faith, obedience, and God's covenant with His people. Here are several specific key themes from his life:

1. Divine Calling and Purpose

One of the central themes in Moses' life is divine calling and purpose. Though born into a time of oppression and placed in a basket to escape death, Moses was chosen by God from the beginning to be a deliverer. His life shows that God's purpose often begins in unlikely circumstances and unfolds in stages. Moses' life follows three 40-year key stages: from the palace, to the desert, to the mountain.

2. Transformation in Leadership

Closely related to the previous point is the theme of leadership transformation. Moses doubted his own abilities when God called him from the burning bush. He objected, feared public speaking, and questioned his worth, yet God used him powerfully. This reminds us that ***God equips those He calls, not necessarily those who already seem equipped***.

3. Intercession and Compassion

Another key theme is intercession and compassion. Moses repeatedly stands in the gap for the people of Israel, pleading with God to show mercy after they rebel, worship idols, or complain. Time and time again! I commend Moses' compassion and patience for the Israelites. His role as a mediator is a type and shadow of and foreshadows the idea of a greater intercessor: Jesus Christ as our Mediator in Heaven.

4. Covenant and Law

Moses' role as mediator at Sinai defined his legacy. Moses stood as the mediator between God and Israel, basking in the presence and glory of God, receiving the Ten Commandments, and copying down the broader Mosaic Law. This covenant both established moral guidelines and stood as a sacred, holy agreement through which God set Israel apart as His chosen people. These laws shaped every aspect of Israel's life, from ethics to worship, and emphasized God's desire for holiness, purity, obedience, and intimacy with His people. Moses' role in delivering and teaching the law would echo throughout Israel's history and ultimately point forward to the New Covenant fulfilled in Jesus Christ.

5. Obedience and Consequences

Moses' story also explores the theme of obedience and consequences. Though he was deeply faithful, even Moses himself faced consequences for his disobedience, specifically, when he struck the rock instead of speaking to it, and was therefore barred from entering the Promised Land. This illustrates God's holiness and the weight of leadership responsibility. Those God calls into levels of leadership are held to higher standards of obedience.

6. God's Presence and Glory

From the divine rescue from the Nile river, being placed in Pharaoh's palace, fleeing into the wilderness, being called from the burning bush, and everything beyond that, Moses was drawn into a journey defined by divine encounter. On Mount Sinai, he ascended into the cloud of God's glory and received the law amid thunder and fire, demonstrating God's holiness and majesty. Very few others in the Bible and throughout history have encountered God's glory as Moses did. In the wilderness, Moses regularly entered the tent of meeting—the very presence of God—where the Lord would speak to him *"face to face, as one speaks to a friend"* (Exodus 33:11). His intercessory prayers for the people of Israel often invited God's continued presence among the people – even when the people as a whole were in the wrong. When he boldly asked, *"Show me your glory"* (Exodus 33:18), revealing a heart hungry not just for guidance, but for God Himself. Even his face physically radiated with God's glory after spending so much time in God's presence (Exodus 34:29–35). Throughout his leadership, Moses served as a mediator, a profound leader, and a vessel of divine glory, showing that God's presence and glory are the trustworthy source of power, direction, and identity for His people.

Pause on the Path

The wilderness is not a place of punishment! It's a place of *preparation*. For Moses, it was not the palace of Pharaoh but the backside of a barren desert where God began to shape his heart for holy leadership. Before Moses could deliver Israel, God had to deliver *Moses* from self-reliance, fear, and the illusion that his life had been wasted.

When Moses fled Egypt, he likely thought his story was over. He had gone from a prince of Egypt to a despised shepherd, from influence to isolation. It's important to note that the wilderness was never meant to be the *end* of his story! It was the very classroom where he learned to recognize the sound of God's voice. The quiet hills of Midian became the training ground for divine encounter. There, away from the busyness and noise of Egypt and slavery, God was preparing His servant in secret. In the wilderness, God took Moses and redefined his identity. He does the same with us! It's where He turns our striving into surrender to His will and purpose. God divinely orchestrates the barren seasons to bloom into fresh identity and relationship.

After forty years in the wilderness, Moses met God at the burning bush. Everything that once looked like failure in Moses' eyes all of a sudden became fuel for the very calling God appointed for him at his birth. The forty years he thought were wasted were actually years of shaping that God *knew he needed*. Every lonely step in the desert had been leading him to the holy ground at the burning bush.

If you find yourself in a wilderness season right now, where doors are closed, prayers feel unanswered, or dreams seem delayed, **take heart**. You are not forgotten or abandoned. You are being formed. God often hides His greatest work in the hidden places that feel like wilderness seasons. It's in the wilderness where God grows roots of humility, endurance, and trust! Those must be grown in us before the fruit of purpose ever begins to appear.

Putting It into Practice

Write: Reflect on your own wilderness seasons—times when you felt unseen or stuck, or circumstances felt uncertain. How did God use those times to draw you closer to Him or to prepare you for something ahead? Journal about what He might be forming in you right now, even if you can't yet see it.

Pray: Ask God to open your eyes to the purpose amidst your present wilderness. Pray that you would trust His timing and refining work, believing that He's preparing you for something greater. Invite His presence into the places that feel dry or desolate.

Act: Instead of trying to escape the season you're in, choose to meet God in it. Spend time alone with Him this week—away from distractions— listening for His voice.

Encourage someone else walking through a "desert place," reminding them that God's presence often shines brightest in solitude.

Worship: Read Exodus 3:4–5 aloud: *"When the LORD saw that he turned aside to see, God called to him out of the bush, 'Moses, Moses!' And he said, 'Here I am.' Then He said, 'Do not come near; take your sandals off your feet, for the place on which you are standing is holy ground.'"* Sing a song that celebrates God's nearness in the wilderness and His ability to make even dry ground holy.

Prayer for the Journey

Lord, thank You for meeting me in the wilderness. Teach me to see beauty where I've only seen barrenness. Help me trust that the waiting and the quiet are part of Your preparation. Strip away what distracts me so I can hear Your voice clearly. I surrender my heart, my mind, and my will to You! Let my wilderness become a place of worship, where fear fades and faith grows. I submit my timetable to You and choose to rest in Your perfect timing. Make this season holy ground under my feet. In Jesus' name, Amen.

CHAPTER 8
Joshua: The Courage to Conquer

Every great story of faith begins in the ordinary: where daily obedience prepares a heart for an extraordinary calling. Before Joshua ever led armies, parted rivers, or claimed promises, he first learned to submit, to serve, and to follow. His story is a striking portrait of what it looks like when quiet faithfulness meets divine opportunity. Throughout his life, we see that God's most outstanding leaders are not born from platforms of prestige but forged in seasons of preparation with humble obedience.

Joshua also had to endure long seasons of waiting for his promise. As Moses' personal assistant, Joshua was present at Mt. Sinai, at the approach to the Promised Land, and during the forty years of wandering after Israel's unbelief. He was one of the two spies who had the faith to believe that God would allow the Israelites to conquer the giants of Canaan. He was a man of strong faith, and yet, he was forced to live in forty years of wilderness wanderings because of the unbelief of ten *other* men who led the entirety of Israel to fear and doubt. Ouch. Talk about a raw deal.

Here's a hard reality: God leads His servants on a powerful, but unconventional path, from obscurity to obedience, through trial to triumph, and finally into legacy. Joshua's story is no different! His victories were not the result of perfect strategy, but perfect *surrender, even when he didn't understand the waiting period.*

As you read Joshua's story, look for yourself within it. We each will face difficult circumstances, like the Jordan River to cross and the high walls of Jericho, where we must trust God through it all. Joshua's life reminds us that *every act of servant obedience—no matter how small—moves us one step closer to the fulfillment of God's plan.* The same God who led Joshua into promise is writing courageous faith and victory into your own divine plotline today.

Joshua's Journey

Joshua's story is told primarily in the book of Joshua (and partly in Numbers and Deuteronomy). As Moses' successor and leader of Israel into the Promised Land, Joshua's life also follows The Hero's Journey with *precision* – another demonstration of God's story archetype being from *His* all-powerful hand. You can find the detailed outline of his Hero's Journey in Appendix 5 at the back of the book.

Joshua began as a Hebrew slave in Egypt. After the Exodus, he became Moses' assistant. Joshua lived among the Israelites during the forty years of wilderness wandering as a military leader (Exodus 17). He is closely connected to Moses, and he even personally encountered God's all-powerful presence on several occasions! After Moses' death, God directly commissioned Joshua to lead the people of Israel into Canaan. The call is bold: *"Be strong and courageous... you will lead these people to inherit the land I promised"* (Joshua 1:6). However, because of the repeated encouragement from God to "not be afraid," it's safe to assume that Joshua still struggled with inner fear or doubt, which God works out of him through his years of growing in leadership.

Joshua faced an immediate test upon entering the Promised Land: he must confront Jericho, a walled city. Instead of a siege, God commanded a strange strategy: marching silently for six days. Joshua was obedient, and God's power brought down Jericho's walls through his obedience. As they progressed into the Promised Land, He dealt with many other tests and trials: failure at Ai due to Achan's secret sin (Joshua 7), the deception of the Gibeonites (who pretended to be allies, Joshua 9), and numerous military conquests, like the battle against the five kings (Joshua 10). He had to discern whom to trust, sought after God's guidance, and united the tribes of Israel in numerous battles. These events taught Joshua to always seek God's guidance *first*.

After defeating the southern and northern kings, much of the Promised Land was subdued (Joshua 10–11). However, full possession and unity remained incomplete. Joshua's most significant test was dividing the land among the tribes (Joshua 13–21), which proved to be challenging emotionally and spiritually, as well as a difficult political endeavor for Joshua. *The challenge was no longer external conquest, but internal peace and unity amongst the people.* Joshua needed to shift from *warrior* to *steward*. Through his faith and reliance on God's wisdom, Joshua succeeded in allotting the land, and Israel had rest from war (Joshua 11:23). His reward was no longer military victory. In its place was wise authority and covenant guardianship.

Near life's end, Joshua gathered Israel's leaders (Joshua 23–24). He reminded Israel of God's laws and called them to commit themselves fully to God. He warned them of the dangers of compromising with foreign nations and gods. Joshua knew that, without continued obedience, their victory would mean nothing.

Joshua's legacy culminated in his final challenge: *"Choose this day whom you will serve… but as for me and my house, we will serve the Lord"* (Joshua 24:15). The people continued to serve the Lord throughout his lifetime. Joshua's journey was one of quiet preparation in humble service, bold faith, hunger for the presence of God, and faithful leadership when God called him. He stepped out of Moses' shadow and into God's purpose. He lead with humble courage and unwavering trust in the Lord. His story shows that heroic leadership often comes through surrender, listening, and obedience — not just bold action.

Be Strong and Courageous

When God spoke to Joshua at the beginning of his commission, He gave him a clear spiritual command: *"Be strong and courageous… for the Lord your God is with you wherever you go"* (Joshua 1:9). And He repeated this sentiment later in the same speech to Joshua! God was calling something out of Joshua: to reject fear and choose the *discipline of courageous dependence on Him.* Joshua's strength would not come from strategic battle plans, expert military training, or even self-confidence! Instead, Joshua's victories would come from the continual awareness of and seeking after God's presence, just as he did at Mt. Sinai and throughout the wilderness wanderings!

Courage, in God's Kingdom, is not the absence of fear. God saw the fear and trepidation within Joshua, which is why He called Joshua to "Be strong and courageous" in the first place! *Courage is the obedience to move forward despite the fear.*

For forty years, Joshua watched a fearful generation shrink back from promise. He saw them reject the promise in fear and complain about the consequences. Once in leadership, God was forming a different spirit in Joshua. God was birthing within Joshua a spirit that trusted more in His divine faithfulness than any human probability. Every step across the Jordan and around Jericho, every act of perseverance required a heart anchored in faith. In the most unlikely of circumstances, Joshua was to walk in courageous obedience.

In the same way, courage today looks less like reckless boldness and more like steadfast obedience. It is the daily choice to say *yes* to God when fear, self-preservation, comfort, or laziness whispers *no*. True courage that honors God and walks in obedience is forged in those daily decisions! When you choose to pray instead of panic, you choose courage. When you choose to forgive that person who so deeply wounded you instead of retaliating, you choose courage. When you obey even when the outcome isn't clear, you choose courage!

Joshua teaches us that *victory always follows surrender.* Spiritual courage doesn't demand that we understand every outcome, only that we trust the One who goes before us, even when the circumstances are hard (or impossible) to understand.

Key Themes from the Life of Joshua

Joshua's story carries and teaches significant themes that have guided generations for the last several thousand years: leadership, faith, obedience, and the fulfillment of God's promises.

1. Courageous Obedience

From the moment God calls him to lead Israel after Moses' death, Joshua is repeatedly told to *"be strong and courageous"* (Joshua 1:6–9), hinting at an underlying fear within him about this new position of leadership. Because of this fear, his story stands as a true model of faith in action: he doesn't just *believe* God's promises; he steps into them *boldly*. Whether he was leading Israel across the Jordan, marching around Jericho, or facing overwhelming armies, Joshua walked in that courageous obedience.

2. Trust in God's Word

Courageous obedience flowed from Joshua's trust in God's promises. Joshua never forgot what God had said to Abraham, Isaac, Jacob, and Moses. His life shows that trusting God's word leads to victorious fulfillment and blessing, even when the odds seem impossible. Over time, Joshua grew from fearful trepidation to unwavering confidence in the Lord and in His Word.

3. Leadership Through Submission

Joshua was not flashy, but faithful. He served Moses in faithful, humble submission for *decades* before ever leading anyone else himself. When his time came, he led with discipline and reliance on God. He was strategic in battle but always sought God's guidance first, demonstrating that *great leadership is rooted in submission to God, not personal power or ability.*

4. Spiritual Legacy

Joshua also embodies covenant renewal and spiritual legacy. At the end of his life, he gathered the people and challenged them to remain faithful to God, famously declaring, *"As for me and my house, we will serve the Lord"* (Joshua 24:15). His leadership didn't just secure military victories; it helped shape the spiritual direction of a generation.

5. Importance of Remembering and Teaching

Finally, a profound theme in Joshua's life is the importance of remembering and teaching. When the Israelites crossed the Jordan, Joshua set up memorial stones so future generations would ask, *"What do these stones mean?"* and hear of God's faithfulness (Joshua 4:21–22). These reminders kept Israel anchored in God's covenant and warned them against drifting into forgetfulness and idolatry. Joshua's life shows us that faith must not only be lived but also passed on, through testimonies, memorials, and intentional teaching, so the next generation would continue to walk with God.

Pause on the Path

Every believer faces a moment when faith must step from belief into practice. For Joshua, that moment came at the edge of the Jordan River. He had spent decades in the shadows. He faithfully served Moses, patiently waiting and believing God's promise even when others refused to do the same. And when the time finally came to lead, God's first command wasn't about battle strategy. It was about *heart posture*: *"Be strong and courageous... for the LORD your God is with you wherever you go"* (Joshua 1:9). Joshua's courage was formed in the forty years of waiting, in the quiet of obedience, and in the ache of seeing others' fear delay *his* destiny. He learned that courage means to *keep walking with God even in the midst of fear*.

Like Joshua, you may be standing on the banks of your own Jordan or at your own walls of Jericho staring at an impossible situation, unsure of what obedience will require. Remember: **courage is trusting His Word even when logic fails.** It's marching around your Jericho even when nothing seems to move. The courage that conquers begins in the heart that refuses to lose faith before it can ever get on the battlefield! And just as God's presence went before Joshua, it goes before you, too!

So, when you face your next step, remember that *victory follows surrender.* God doesn't need your perfection; He wants your persistent faith and willing obedience.

Putting It into Practice

Write: What "Jordan" or "Jericho" stands before you right now? What step of faith feels risky or impossible? Write down your fears about addressing it, then write God's promise beside each one. Replace every lie of inadequacy with the truth of His presence. Find Bible verses to specifically combat the lies trying to hold you back.

Pray: Ask God to increase and renew your courage. Pray for the discipline to obey even when it's uncomfortable, and the endurance to wait well when His timing feels delayed.

Act: Take one practical step of obedience this week—no matter how small. It might be initiating a challenging conversation, stepping into a new ministry, forgiving someone, or starting something God's been nudging you toward. Step out, trusting that God will meet you halfway across the Jordan.

Worship: Read Joshua 3:5 aloud: *"Consecrate yourselves, for tomorrow the LORD will do amazing things among you."* Sing a song of trust and expectation, praising God for the miracles He's preparing on the other side of your obedience.

Prayer for the Journey

Father, thank You for walking with me into every unknown. I know and believe that you have never left me to the unknown! Teach me to trust Your presence more than any fear I feel. Give me courage that obeys even when I don't understand and faith that endures even when the waiting feels long. Just as You went before Joshua, go before me! Part every river, tear down every wall, and guide my every step. I choose to be strong and courageous, not because I am fearless, but because You are faithful. In Jesus' name, Amen.

CHAPTER 9

David: The Crown Forged in the Cave

During the time of the Judges, the people of Israel wavered between being faithful to the Lord and worshipping the idols of the surrounding nations. This broke God's heart. Though He raised leaders like Deborah, Gideon, and Samson to bring them back, the people continued to rebel. Eventually, they demanded a king to rule them, rejecting God's direct leadership.

When God agreed to their demand, He already knew the outcome, and He purposed to use even their rebellion to fulfill His plan. Out of obscurity, He raised up David, a shepherd boy who—through tremendous trials and challenges—would become Israel's greatest king and the one He called *"a man after My own heart"* (1 Samuel 13:14 and Acts 13:22).

What's remarkable is that God gave David this title *before* he faced Goliath, wore a crown, or wrote the Psalms. God recognized that David was the man He needed to lead His people and start this new Kingdom. There was already within him a heart hungry for God's leadership. But this raises a question: if God had already chosen David to serve him with his whole heart, why allow him to walk through years of wilderness, betrayal, and hiding for his life? I'm glad you asked! The answer lies in God's refining process—The Hero's Journey of growth and transformation. Even hearts devoted to God must be tested, strengthened, and matured so they can carry the weight of the calling God places on them.

The Secret Ingredient for Effective Leadership

As we saw in Joshua's story, he shared a similar beginning to David. Both men *already* earnestly desired the things of God, and yet, they still endured years of hardship before they took their position of leadership. Their lives show us that even when we're doing all the "right things," God knows what trials we must walk through to prepare our hearts for His purposes.

Suffering and hardship remain some of God's most effective tools for shaping servant-leaders. We've seen this truth in the lives of Job, Abraham, Joseph, Moses, and Joshua, and it continues in David's life. This isn't a topic that most Christians like to discuss, but I believe it's something we *should all be talking about*. Suffering, hardship, trials, calamities, struggles - all of these are God's secret ingredient. When this secret ingredient is missing in a leader's life, leadership almost always corrupts the heart.

Two clear examples of this Biblical truth lie in the two kings who bookend David's life: Saul and Solomon. Both of these men were given their positions of leadership without undergoing any Biblically documented Hero's Journey. And their reigns ended with tragedy and apostasy!

Saul was chosen to be king because he was tall and handsome – a foolish standard for leadership, as I once learned in my own life. But I digress! Saul was anointed king and, because of that anointing from God, the Lord's favor rested upon him. He began successfully and went on to overcome the Israelite enemies in many strategic battles. However, as his leadership and authority grew, so did Saul's pride. Eventually, he no longer feared the Lord. He sinned greatly by playing the part of a priest without holding the ordained office of the priest. His arrogance was his downfall and cost him the throne. What was Saul missing? He never walked through The Hero's Journey before he stepped into his position of leadership and authority.

Similarly, Solomon, David's son with Bathsheba, also missed the secret ingredient of effective leadership by missing the crucial Hero's Journey. God had compassion on David after his affair with Bathsheba and the murder of Uriah because David showed such sincere, immediate repentance. God promised David that Bathsheba's next son would be the king after him. Solomon was born into privilege in the palace of Israel as the king's favored son. On his deathbed, David designated Solomon as the next king, and Solomon began his reign.

Shortly after his coronation, God offered Solomon anything he wanted. Solomon asked for divine wisdom. God delivered, and Solomon is still considered one of the wisest men of history. Although he initially served the Lord, his *pride* and *lack of fear of the Lord* eventually led him into idolatry. (On a side note, it's interesting to note here that those are also the sins that corrupted the heart of Lucifer and caused his fall from Heaven). The secret ingredient of wilderness struggles resulted in tragedy for him and Israel.

As you can see in these two examples, when people are placed in leadership positions *without* enduring the trials and heartache of The Hero's Journey, they tragically fall short of the Lord's calling on their lives. By contrast, David's path was marked by betrayal, attempted murder, wilderness exile, and years of waiting. For years, he endured all of these trials before he was able to take his place on the throne of Israel – despite *already* being the anointed king of Israel! God had called him, but he still had to be refined before taking the throne. Even after taking the throne of Israel, David still stumbled into grievous sins! However, unlike Saul and Solomon, his years of trial had shaped him into a man who was quick to humble himself and repent.

My Journey in God's Secret Ingredient of Suffering

I can relate to David's growth in leadership after he walked through his Hero's Journey (which I'll explain in the next section). After graduating with my Bachelor's in Music Industry and later a Master's in Education, I was confident in my abilities as a vocalist and leader. I taught vocal lessons at the university level, volunteered as a vocalist at my church, and felt very secure in my gifts. But beneath the surface, I lived in pride and hidden sin. I entered the workforce as a public school teacher and, soon after, met my first husband.

From 2016 to 2023, God walked me through my own wilderness journey. During this time, I walked through an abusive marriage, the birth of my first child, COVID lockdowns, leaving my then-husband, divorce proceedings, fear of losing my child, rejection from a previous church's leadership, being on the receiving end of immense slander, and - most of all - tremendous humbling. Through it all, I clung to God. He knew exactly how to break down my pride and reshape my heart.

After all of that, I returned to the church I grew up in (this is when Pastor Jenni and I reconnected). After a few years of attending Life Bible Church, I humbled myself and asked Pastor Jenni if she would allow me to serve on the worship team again. After the rejection I received due to my divorce from the previous church, I was very nervous to ask to help serve again at Life Bible. However, Pastor Jenni was gracious and welcomed me back on the team with love and forgiveness. I expected to be placed as a background vocalist, as I felt like I deserved nothing more. Instead, Pastor Jenni placed me as a worship co-leader. Humbled and shocked, I saw God's grace in action. Over the next two years, under Pastor Jenni's mentorship, I grew in leadership. She asked me to become the church's private vocal coach, to become a worship co-leader, to start *and lead* the church's monthly praise choir, and even her personal editor for her sermon and class notes.

Where I had once desired leadership and recognition for all the wrong reasons, I was now placed in a leadership position without asking for it. God always knew where He needed to tenderize my heart, and He walked me through the exact journey to get me there. The journey was *arduous* for me, and it is still hard at times! The wilderness softened my heart toward the Lord, the Church, and worship itself. Now, every time I enter into a time of worship, it melts my heart in a way that I had never experienced before as I walk through my wilderness journey. When I lead worship or direct choir, my heart is undone by God's presence. In my vocal coaching, I also teach the church's worship leaders how to use their bodies and voices most effectively to present a living sacrifice of praise, to deliver the songs of the Lord, and to lead the congregation into the Throneroom of Heaven. The fruit I see from my students astounds and humbles me immensely. The Lord has used my wilderness season to bring me into a place of leadership that I still have a hard time wrapping my mind around! Like I said: humbling and astounding.

Like David, my trials became the secret ingredient in my life for fruitful leadership – and I'm just seeing the beginnings of the fruit! I never expected to co-lead worship, teach other vocalists, or even write this very book—but here I am! I won't lie to you when I say that I'm actually excited to see all that God will do with my life and how He will use the suffering seasons of my life (and all future sufferings) to propel me further into His purposes. I've learned that God always works *"...all things together for good, for those who are called according to his purpose"* (Romans 8:28). Because of that, I no longer dread future hardships—they actually make me eager to see how God will use them for His glory and my transformation.

David's Journey

As for David, his life is another perfect example of The Hero's Journey and how God uses it to mature and tenderize the hearts of His people for His purposes. He began as the youngest son of Jesse, a shepherd in Bethlehem (1 Samuel 16:11). His world was quiet and obscure—tending sheep, writing psalms, and playing music—far removed from Israel's political turmoil.

David's simple life is abruptly interrupted when the prophet Samuel comes to his house. David was chosen by Samuel and anointed as the future king of Israel (1 Samuel 16:13), which was an act of treason against King Saul. Though the Spirit of the Lord came upon him, David had to wait and suffer for years before receiving the crown. *(Remember the secret ingredient?)*

David's life, although already changed when anointed by Samuel, changed even more drastically when he challenged and defeated Goliath (1 Samuel 17). This act propelled him into national fame and favor, military leadership, and Saul's household. It also made him a threat in the king's eyes.

David endured numerous trials and tests, such as navigating Saul's growing hatred, avoiding assassination attempts, navigating the confusion of mutiny from his followers, and choosing mercy over revenge (cutting Saul's robe, sparing his life), and more! In the many trials, *he had to remain faithful, wise, and innocent – even as he was hunted unjustly.*

David's journey took a dark and morally complicated turn when, exhausted from years of running, he sought refuge among Israel's sworn enemies: the Philistines. Though he outwardly aligned with the Philistines, David secretly raided Israel's enemies to stay in God's favor. This dual life reveals David's deep, internal tension between survival and faith.

This was the deepest phase of isolation, moral tension, and identity crisis. However, God intervened on David's behalf by turning the four other kings of the Philistines against him, giving him a way out of the position of compromise he found himself in.

David's greatest personal crisis came when the Amalekites raided, burned the city, and captured his men's families. His own followers, broken and angry, spoke of mutiny and stoning David. At this moment of utter despair, David turned to his foundation: he *"strengthened himself in the Lord his God"* (1 Samuel 30:6). Instead of collapsing, he sought divine guidance, rallied his men, and recovered everything that had been taken.

Following his triumph at Ziklag and the death of Saul in battle, David finally steps into a measure of kingship, a reward for the wilderness season he had just walked through. However, he did not rush to claim power but chose to seek God's will *first*. Upon his return and anointing as king of Judah, he began to rule from Hebron.

Though the full promise had not yet come to pass, David finally held legitimate authority and led with patience and wisdom, which was developed through the wilderness waiting. He waited in hope and faith for God to bring about the unification of the kingdom at God's perfect timing, refusing to grasp at power prematurely or to take advantage of Saul's fallen house. He reigned over Judah for seven and a half years before moving further into the purposes of God. It is estimated that David had to wait approximately *fifteen years* from the moment he was first anointed the king of Israel until he was *actually* able to become king of Judah.

Finally, David became king of all Israel. He took Jerusalem and made it the center of both political authority and spiritual worship, bringing the ark of the covenant into the city. This moment symbolized the rebirth of David's calling, no longer as a fugitive or tribal leader, but as the shepherd-king of all Israel, refined by suffering and elevated by God's hand.

David's reign brought unity and justice, as well as the centrality of worship in Israel. God made an everlasting covenant with him, promising his line would endure forever. David's kingdom was shaped by divine favor, righteous leadership, and messianic hope—one that ultimately points forward to Jesus, the true Son of David.

Key Themes from David's Journey

Although an ancient true story, David's journey from humble shepherd to king of Israel touches on many rich spiritual and theological depths that can directly apply to our lives today. His story demonstrates the "living and active" power of God's Word. Here are the key themes of David's life that have impacted and encouraged me the most, as I have walked through my wilderness journey:

1. God's Sovereign Choice

David's life highlights the truth that God chooses people—not based on outward appearance or political status—but on the heart. Even as Samuel was looking at the six sons of Jesse initially present at the sacrifice, God quietly reminded Samuel that *"... The LORD sees not as man sees: man looks on the outward appearance, but the LORD looks on the heart"* (1 Samuel 16:7b). Long before David's name was even introduced, God had declared, *"The Lord has sought out a man after his own heart"* (1 Samuel 13:14). That man was David! God, through Samuel, anointed David as King and used His lineage to bring about the Savior and Messiah of the World! David's story beautifully reinforces the theme that God exalts the humble and opposes the proud.

2. Faith in God's Power

David exercised extraordinary, tenacious faith. Even as a shepherd boy, he exercised his faith by fighting off lions and bears to protect his flocks. David's victory over Goliath demonstrated this same radical faith in God rather than any human strength - including his own. His courage flowed from deep intimacy with God, cultivated in hidden places of worship and prayer. After the anointing of the Lord came upon him by the prophet Samuel, David's faith grew as he trusted in the Lord's deliverance when all others cowered in fear. This theme of courageous, God-centered faith is central to his life—from his shepherding season to his trials in the wilderness, and continued through his leadership as king. Though imperfect, David was quick to repent and return to God's presence, always seeking to walk in His favor.

3. God's Presence and Intimacy

David was "a man after God's own heart." His psalms reveal a deep personal relationship with the Lord. He experienced God not just as King or Deliverer, but as Shepherd, Refuge, Rock, and Father. His psalms are filled with raw emotion, humility, and honesty, and serve as a true reflection of intimacy. In his psalms, which are a glimpse into his secret thought life, we see a man so close to the Lord that he was willing to pour out every thought and emotion at the feet of the Father - knowing full well that none of it would scare or hinder God away from him. From lonely pastures to the palace, David cultivated intimacy with God through both triumph and trial, showing us that true worship flows from a deep relationship.

4. Patience in the Midst of Delay

Though anointed as king in his youth, David still had to wait approximately fifteen years before ascending the throne of Judah, and another seven and a half years before his coronation as king of all Israel. During that time, he endured fear, betrayal, exile, and near death, but he chose to wait on God's timing rather than seize power through violence. We see David confess a few times that God's plan is always right and perfect:

1. When David spared Saul in the cave at En Gedi (1 Samuel 24:10).

2. When David spared Saul's life **again** at Hakilah Hill (1 Samuel 26:9–10).

3. When David mourned Saul's death, instead of celebrating it (2 Samuel 1:23).

4. When David inquired of the Lord before moving forward after Saul's death (2 Samuel 2:1).

5. When David waited another seven and a half years to rule all Israel (2 Samuel 5:5).

David's life was marked by this truth: **God's promises are true, but His timing is *holy*.** David consistently modeled his unwavering belief in this principle. He lived with such restraint, reverence, and dependence on God's timing, never short-cutting the process, even when that meant he would suffer longer than he might ever have wanted. Wow! If you take anything away from the life of David, let it be this key theme from his life: God's promises are true, but His timing is *holy*.

5. Leadership Shaped by Suffering

David's years in the wilderness were NOT a waste; they prepared him for kingship. It was in the wilderness that he learned to lead, to forgive, to seek God, and to rely on the Lord for strength and provision. His story strongly and clearly reminds us that **God often forms leaders in obscurity and hardship** before elevating them to public influence. The same truth applies to us: the days, weeks, months, or years in the wilderness *are not a waste!* This season is where God will do his most outstanding writing and most significant development in each of us. He will *never* waste the wilderness suffering.

6. The Importance of Worship

From his years as a young shepherd to his time as king of Israel, David was a worshiper at heart. He wrote many of the Psalms throughout his life, organized temple worship, established Mount Zion (a fresh revelation of worship), and brought the Ark of the Covenant to Jerusalem. Many of his psalms reveal the inner workings of David's thought life, portraying his emotions—good and bad—and how he expressed them to the Lord. Even after he is crowned king of all Israel, we still see a strong love of worship in David's heart! He worshiped unapologetically before the Lord, so much so that it ended up costing his wife, Michal, her fertility as she harshly judged David's outward expression of worship (2 Samuel 6:16-23)! Coming out of immense pain and suffering, David worshipped with fresh fervor and intimacy that could only come from that place. His example of unhindered (or, as David calls it, "undignified") worship shows that **leadership rooted in worship draws people toward God**, not toward themselves.

7. Brokenness and Restoration

David's life was marked by tragedy even in his family: his daughter, Tamar's, assault by his son, Amnon (2 Samuel 13); his son, Absalom's, rebellion and usurpation (2 Samuel 15–18); and the death of his infant son by Bathsheba after their affair (2 Samuel 12:15–18). Despite these heartbreaking failures of David's story – even after becoming king of Israel – David continued to seek the Lord. His life reflects the reality that **God's purposes can still unfold through flawed, broken people**.

Pause on the Path

David's journey shows that a heart for God matters more than outward strength or status. He was called from a young age, without any significant accomplishments or reputation. Remember, he wasn't even considered to be called from the fields when Samuel came to meet the sons of Jesse! Yet,

God called him out of obscurity and set him on a wild adventure. He faced giants, encountered heartbreak, experienced betrayal, led victorious armies, dealt with mutiny from his men, and, after years of wilderness wanderings, finally encountered his promised inheritance from the Lord and ruled a kingdom. Despite his victories and failures, his story reminds us that God's mercy restores and renews those who genuinely seek Him.

In our own lives, it's easy to get overwhelmed by hardships and frustrations. Let's be real: life is full of pain, disappointment, broken hearts, and delayed promises. When you find yourself in a season of trials, don't lose heart. Go to the Psalms and read David's raw outpourings before the Lord. David unleashed his emotions and struggled with honesty—and God *still* called him a "man after God's own heart." Pour out your heart before the Lord in complete surrender and remember: your God is the God of giant-slaying and great victories. Even if the outcome looks different from what you hoped for, God is still at work. Keep pressing into Him and seeking His purposes in your life, just as David did.

Putting It into Practice

Write: Take time to journal one season when you were in a "wilderness" like David — a time of waiting, running, or being misunderstood. Write down how God used that season to shape your trust in Him. Then, note how you saw His promises fulfilled over time.

Pray: Confess any words you may have spoken out of fear or anger towards the Lord in times of trials and heartbreak. Repent of those things and ask God to reveal Himself to you - even in the most challenging times. Pray through a Psalm of David (e.g., Psalm 23, 27, or 63), making it your own. Thank God for His faithfulness in both valleys and mountaintops. Ask Him to help you trust His timing, even when the "throne" He's promised feels far away.

Act: Identify one "giant" you are facing — a challenge, fear, or sin. Write it down, then in prayer, symbolically "place it" into God's hands. This week, take one practical step forward in faith, trusting Him to fight for you.

Like David, let worship become your weapon. Create a short list of songs, hymns, or Scripture readings that you can return to when discouragement strikes. Use them to re-center your heart on God's character, not your circumstances.

Find someone in your life who is in a "waiting" season. Share with them a personal testimony of God's faithfulness from your own wilderness. Remind them that God's delays are never denials, and that His anointing comes with His perfect timing.

Prayer for the Journey

Lord, give me a heart that seeks You above all else. Like David, I want my heart to seek You above all others. I long to be used by You, even if that means walking through a wilderness season. Lord, I trust You and Your outcomes. I know that You know best! I know Your plans are far above and beyond anything I could imagine. Help me keep my eyes off my wilderness season and stay focused on You, who will be with me through it all. I trust Your molding and maturing process. Break me of all pride that would lead me to believe that "I know best." Keep me humble throughout it all! I surrender my wilderness season to Your masterful pen, Lord. In Jesus' name, Amen.

CHAPTER 10

Paul: When Misplaced Zeal Meets Transforming Grace

In my writing journey, when I transitioned from the Old Testament into the New Testament, I faced the challenge of choosing which lives to highlight as evidence of The Hero's Journey in the Bible. The New Testament is full of people whose stories reflect this divine pattern: Mother Mary, Matthew, Peter, John the disciple of Jesus, John the Baptist, Mary Magdalene, Lazarus, Zacchaeus, the Samaritan woman at the well, Timothy, Onesimus, Cornelius, and even *Jesus* Himself! Each of their stories stands as an astounding testament to God's consistent use of this perfect story structure and to His effective writing in molding and transforming His children for His glory.

Yet among all of these, none astonishes me quite like the Apostle Paul. His radical transformation makes his story one of the strongest examples of God's divine plotline! That being said, I would encourage you to dive into and study the lives in the list above! You will be amazed to see how God really does use His perfect, consistent, transformative storyline in each of their lives.

It's worth noting a common misconception about his name here. Even after his conversion, Saul continued to go by his Hebrew name, *Saul*, for some time. He didn't start going by the name *Paul* until he began his missionary work to the Gentiles in Acts 13:9 *("Then Saul, who was also called Paul...")*. *Saul* was his name in Hebrew, but *Paul* was his name in Latin. So, the name Saul would've been more akin to a Jewish audience, while the name Paul would've fit better for his missionary travels to the Gentiles. It's a common belief that "Paul" was his "new name" after his conversion, but that's actually not true. The shift was practical, not symbolic of a new identity.

Paul's Early Life

Paul is first mentioned in the Bible as a zealous, prideful Pharisee named "Saul" shortly after Jesus' death and resurrection. However, we really don't know very much about him or his early life. We know he was born in Tarsus as a Roman citizen. We know that he was a zealous adherent of Jewish law and customs (as he says of himself in Philippians 3:5-6). He was actively leading the persecution of the followers of Jesus, as he believed them to be heretics. We see this a few times throughout Acts 7-9:

> **Acts 7:57-58** – *"At this, they covered their ears and, yelling at the top of their voices, they all rushed at him, dragged him out of the city, and began to stone him. Meanwhile, the witnesses laid their coats at the feet of a young man named **Saul**."*
>
> **Acts 8:1–3** – *"**Saul** was ravaging the church... entering house after house, he dragged off men and women and committed them to prison."*
>
> **Acts 9:1** – *"**Saul**, still breathing threats and murder against the disciples of the Lord. He went to the high priest and asked him for letters to the synagogues in Damascus, so that if he found any there who belonged to the Way, whether men or women, he might take them as prisoners to Jerusalem."*

These accounts also show Saul's influence: the high priest entrusted him with official letters to arrest believers in Damascus (Acts 9:2). This suggests Saul held significant authority and status among the Pharisees. Saul was no "shmuck!" He was well-known, reputable, successful, pious, religious, and dedicated. From the Jewish community, he would've been doing all the *right* things, devoted to serving the Lord.

When God Overturns Misguided Righteousness

Looking back, it's easy for us to see Saul as a murderous villain. But in his mind, he was defending God's honor and protecting Israel from dangerous false teaching. That's what makes his transformation so astonishing. Now, we know how wrong he was because we know that Jesus really is the Christ, but I think sometimes we need to stop and consider things from Saul's perspective. He wasn't a man openly rebelling against God – he *thought* he was serving Him. Until, of course, God radically intervened and turned his life upside down. In *his eyes,* Paul's story is one of a man who was doing "all the right things" until God radically turned his life upside down, spun it around, sent him on a wild ride into the unknown, and brought all the humbling along the way.

Now, I am sure your backstory may not be as extreme as Paul's, but can I challenge you with something? Maybe you can relate to Paul in a way? Perhaps you've spent much of your life dedicated to the Lord and His purposes? Perhaps you grew up in church, or maybe you're a pastor's kid, or even a pastor yourself?! Possibly you feel like you've made the right choices: you've served the Lord, dedicated time to Him every day, read your Bible frequently, and prayed daily. You have lived your life to honor Him in all things, and yet you've found yourself in a situation similar to Saul's: your life turned in an unknown direction, with no end in sight?

Many of us in the church sincerely believe we are doing "all the right things" for the Lord. We serve, we give, we attend, we even speak His name with confidence. But the truth is that God measures things differently than we do. God is not impressed by our activities; He searches the hidden motives of our hearts. Too often, what we celebrate as righteousness is, in reality, contaminated by pride, self-reliance, misguided theology, or shallow tradition. I know this is hard to hear, but please understand that this is coming from a heart that loves you and cares about your growth, your transformation, and your freedom in Christ—and from someone who has dealt with this in her own life. The prophet Isaiah reminds us plainly: *"...All our righteous deeds are like a polluted garment...."* (Isaiah 64:6a). When we elevate our own "goodness" above intimacy with God and obedience to His Word, we risk falling into the same trap that Saul did: mistaking outward zeal for inward devotion.

Church, this is not a light matter. The danger is real! When we elevate our own "good things" above the sincere pursuit of God Himself, we deceive ourselves and risk misrepresenting Him to the world. Pride disguised as holiness is deadly. We must repent of performance-driven religion and return to the place of humility, trembling before His Word, before we repeat the error of Saul.

On the flip side, maybe you have found yourself serving God your whole life from a sincere and genuine heart. Job's life followed a similar pattern: though he lived righteously, God allowed him to endure immense suffering for a greater purpose. God did the same thing with Abraham. God did the same thing with many of his servants and saints throughout history. And maybe God is walking you through that same kind of refining journey. If you've found yourself asking, "Why me, Lord? Haven't I been faithful?"—take courage. The same God who transformed Job, Abraham, and Paul is at work in you. He will see His purposes through to completion. Some of the greatest transformative stories of all time have come from humble beginnings, already dedicated to the Lord. Saul's story reminds us that sometimes even those who believe they are walking righteously may need God to dismantle their assumptions and redirect their path.

Paul's Journey

Saul began as a devout Pharisee from Tarsus, well educated from youth, and respected among the religious elite. His life was orderly, respectable, and in alignment with Jewish law. From the casual onlooker, he was doing "all the right things." From God's perspective, Saul was seriously in the wrong! Jesus Himself interrupts Saul as he was traveling to Damascus to arrest any followers of "The Way." Along the road, Saul had a blinding encounter with the Messiah and was invited into a radically new mission: to serve the Jesus he had opposed.

After his call and time of mentorship with Ananias, we see in Acts 9:20 that *"At once he began to preach..."* Saul wasted no time and began preaching that Jesus was the Son of God—a stark contrast to the message he had been carrying on the road to Damascus! Once a persecutor of The Way, he stepped into a new world of evangelism for Jesus!

When Saul stepped away from his Pharisee cohort, he began to face significant opposition. The Jewish leaders must have been enraged that their leader in quelling the rebellion of "The Way" had a sudden and dramatic conversion to the exact "cult" he was sent to persecute! He was met with significant (and well-earned) mistrust from Christians and the apostles as well. And he also faced numerous hardships on his missionary journeys, like stonings, beatings, and imprisonment. Paul actually describes his trials and testings in his second letter to the church in Corinth, when he says:

> "[I have] been in prison more frequently, been flogged more severely, and been exposed to death again and again. Five times I received from the Jews the forty lashes minus one. Three times I was beaten with rods, once I was pelted with stones, three times I was shipwrecked, I spent a night and a day in the open sea, I have been constantly on the move. I have been in danger from rivers, in danger from bandits, in danger from my fellow Jews, in danger from Gentiles; in danger in the city, in danger in the country, in danger at sea; and in danger from false believers. I have labored and toiled and have often gone without sleep; I have known hunger and thirst and have often gone without food; I have been cold and naked" (2 Corinthians 11:23-28).

After some time of missionary work and planting churches, Paul returned to Jerusalem, the stronghold of his fiercest enemies. There, he was arrested, beaten, and accused by the religious leaders until he invoked his Roman citizenship and appealed directly to Caesar. This began an even more difficult season of his journey. Paul endured hearings before Felix, Festus, and Agrippa, years of imprisonment, shipwreck, and near-death experiences – all the while staying faithful to his mission.

When he finally made it to Caesar's court, standing before the empire's most significant authority, Paul's life hung in the balance. Yet, he did not waver. The trial was not simply about his fate — it was about the fate of the Gospel reaching the nations.

If anyone made a positive situation out of terrible circumstances, it was Paul. Despite his chains and imprisonment, Paul chose to write letters to encourage and strengthen the churches he had planted. Paul's reward was greater spiritual influence, clarity of his calling, and an eternal impact that would echo for all time. This is most clearly seen in his letter to the Philippians when he said, *"...I have learned, in whatever situation I am, to be content. I know how to be brought low, and I know how to abound. In any and every circumstance, I have learned the secret of facing plenty and hunger, abundance and need. I can do all things through him who strengthens me"* (Philippians 4:11-13). This was his prize and his reward: Christ who strengthens him. And that truth continues to resound in the mouths of Christians even today.

Instead of returning home, Paul pressed forward with urgency. Knowing his time was short, he poured into building leaders, strengthening churches, and writing letters that would outlive him. The end of Paul's story is unknown; however, he likely died a martyr in Rome. But his words and witness lived on! While Paul continues his eternal existence before the Throne of Heaven, his journey birthed his rich, world-changing writing. These writings became the theological backbone of the church and continue to transform lives worldwide.

His journey brought wisdom, transformation, and truth to generations and stands as another beautiful, clear example of The Hero's Journey as God's divine plotline to refine and transform His saints. God can transform even His fiercest opponent into a vessel of grace. In God's hands, Paul's life became a pathway of **surrender, transformation, and mission**. His journey wasn't about personal glory but about reflecting the glory of Christ. And the fruit of his life is still seen throughout the world today!

Key Themes from the Life of Paul

1. Radical Transformation

Paul's story began with him as Saul of Tarsus, a zealous Pharisee who believed it was his holy duty to stamp out Christianity. He actively persecuted Christians, dragging men and women from their homes and approving of their imprisonment or death (Acts 8:3; Acts 9:1–2). But on the road to Damascus, he was stopped by the risen Jesus, struck blind, and led into the city where his physical sight and, more importantly, his spiritual eyes were opened. This moment reveals to us the transformative power of God's grace. **God didn't wait for Saul to get his act together. He interrupted Saul's violence with mercy and called him by name.** His life embodies the truth he wrote in his second letter to the church in Corinth, when he said, *"If anyone is in Christ, he is a new creation..."* (2 Corinthians 5:17). Paul's story proves that no one is beyond redemption! God's powerful transformation can happen suddenly and thoroughly.

2. Grace Over Legalism

Paul's former identity was rooted in legalism, in which he followed the law to the letter and took pride in his heritage, knowledge, and moral record. After meeting Jesus, he realized righteousness cannot be earned but is given through grace: *"By grace you have been saved... not by works"* (Ephesians 2:8–9). He spent his ministry dismantling legalism and pointing to the Gospel of faith in Jesus. This theme is central to the Gospel he preached: we are saved not by what we do, but by what Christ has done.

3. Calling and Mission

From the moment of his conversion, God declared to Ananias, *"He is my chosen instrument to carry my name before the Gentiles, kings, and Israelites"* (Acts 9:15). His mission wasn't one he sought out! Instead, God chose him specifically. God repurposed the same boldness and drive Saul had previously used to *persecute* the Church and redirected it toward *building* the Church. Through his missionary journeys, church plants, mentoring, and letters, Paul became the New Testament's central voice of theology. His calling reminds us that God uses our past, our personality, and our pain as part of our divine assignment, transforming us through His divine plotline —The Hero's Journey.

4. Suffering and Endurance

Paul's life was far from comfortable after he became a Christian. He was beaten, imprisoned, shipwrecked, betrayed, stoned, and eventually martyred for his faith in Jesus. Yet, he didn't interpret suffering as God's absence, but as a mark of true discipleship. He also writes extensively on how suffering produces perseverance, character, and hope. Here are just a few of those examples:

- Romans 5:3-5 – *"Not only that, but we rejoice in our sufferings, knowing that suffering produces endurance, and endurance produces character, and character produces hope, and hope does not put us to shame, because God's love has been poured into our hearts through the Holy Spirit who has been given to us."*

- Romans 8:18 – *"For I consider that the sufferings of this present time are not worth comparing with the glory that is to be revealed to us."*

- 2 Corinthians 4:8-10 – *"We are afflicted in every way, but not crushed; perplexed, but not driven to despair; persecuted, but not forsaken; struck down, but not destroyed; Always carrying in the body the death of Jesus, so that the life of Jesus may also be manifested in our bodies."*

- Philippians 1:29-30 – *"For it has been granted to you that for the sake of Christ you should not only believe in him but also suffer for his sake, Engaged in the same conflict that you saw I had and now hear that I still have."*

- 2 Timothy 2:3-4 – *"Share in suffering as a good soldier of Christ Jesus. No soldier gets entangled in civilian pursuits, since he aims to please the one who enlisted him."*

5. Power in Weakness

One of the most interesting points Paul makes that has constantly challenged me is Paul's "thorn in the flesh." He mentions this in 2 Corinthians when he said, *"So to keep me from becoming conceited… a thorn was given me in the flesh, a messenger of Satan to harass me, to keep me from becoming conceited. Three times I pleaded with the Lord about this, that it should leave me. But he said to me, 'My grace is sufficient for you, for my power is made perfect in weakness'"* (2 Corinthians 12:7-9a). As a child and young adult, I struggled to understand this verse. However, as an adult who has endured my own journey through hardships and humbling, I have a much richer, personal appreciation for Paul's thorn.

Biblical scholars debate whether Paul's persistent thorn was a physical infirmity/pain, or a relational struggle, such as a challenging person he had to endure. Regardless of which it was, one thing we know for sure: God did not remove the thorn from Paul, even after repeated prayer. Through this remaining, present thorn, Paul learned to rely on God's strength, *not his own*. This theme confronts cultural ideals of self-sufficiency – both in Paul's time *and* in our era today! Paul teaches us that true power lies not in human ability but in humble dependence. In our weakness, God's glory and power are more clearly seen.

6. Unity in the Body of Christ

As a Jew called to preach to Gentiles, Paul broke down walls of division. Paul followed in the footsteps of Jesus and brought the truth of the Gospel to the Gentile world. His letters consistently urge the Church to overcome division (of the Jew vs. Gentile variety) and embrace unity, looking past the differences of old and looking forward to unity in

Christ. Paul teaches, *"There is neither Jew nor Greek... for you are all one in Christ"* (Galatians 3:28) and further reiterated this in 1 Corinthians 12:12–27, when he teaches on the numerous parts of the body of Christ – all different, but all valuable and necessary. In a time of deep ethnic, class, religious, and gender divisions, Paul advocated for radical oneness rooted in the Spirit. His teaching laid the foundation for a new identity: not based on background, but on belonging to Christ.

7. Faith and Justification

Paul was the primary voice in the New Testament articulating this doctrine: we are justified—declared righteous—through our faith in Jesus alone, not by any works. His teachings on this subject are one reason why some Biblical scholars credit Paul with writing the book of Hebrews, in which this theme echoes. His writings in Romans and Galatians clarify this central truth of the gospel:

- Romans 3:28 – *"We hold that one is justified by faith apart from works."*

- Galatians 2:16 – *"A person is not justified by the works of the law..."*

Paul didn't just teach this concept. He lived it. He experienced firsthand the freeing power of faith in Jesus when he was set free from the endless treadmill of striving for righteousness and rested in the finished work of Christ.

8. Hope in Suffering and Death

Paul's writings overflow with *hope*. For Paul, it didn't seem to matter what he was facing; he faced it with hope. In Philippians, Paul explained to the church that he saw either death or life as a victory for him! He said, *"For to me to live is Christ, and to die is gain. If I am to live in the flesh, that means fruitful labor for me. Yet which I shall choose I cannot tell. I am hard-pressed between the two. I desire to depart and be with Christ, for that is far better. But to remain in the flesh is more necessary on your account"* (Philippians 1:21-24). This core belief is further reiterated later in the same letter when he said, *"...I have learned, in whatever situation I am, to be content. I know how to be brought low, and I know how to abound. In any and every circumstance, I have learned the secret of facing plenty and hunger, abundance and need. I can do all things through him who strengthens me"* (Philippians 4:11-13). Paul saw death not as the end but the beginning of eternity with Christ. His hope was anchored beyond this life, and it allowed him to face martyrdom without fear. Whether facing hunger, shipwreck, beatings, hatred, persecution, isolation, or impending death, he expressed hope through peace and joy and held every confidence in God's ultimate victory.

Pause on the Path

Paul's life displays the radical transformation possible through an encounter with Christ. Remember, from Saul's perspective, he was doing the "right thing" by persecuting the Christians. It's tough to see change and conviction from someone who genuinely thinks they are doing the right thing! However, God enabled him to go from zealous persecutor to tireless missionary through one encounter with Jesus. *That's* the power of the God we serve! Paul's Hero's Journey was fueled by God-given grace from the moment Jesus first met him on that road. Because of the call of God on His life, Paul's hardships—the beatings, imprisonments, stonings, shipwrecks, near-death experiences, persecution, and rejection—became a platform for the Gospel's advance throughout the world! God used Paul's hardships to catapult him into radical transformation, enabling him to walk out in total obedience to the will of God.

His life stands as a testament to this truth: *You can use your hardships as momentum, not as hindrances, for your calling.* We can look at Paul's life and be assured: your life doesn't have to look perfect to be used by God. You don't have to have everything "all figured out"—a decent house, a stable career, a happy homelife, good health, or a picturesque family — to be used by God. Paul experienced tremendous difficulties, but God used them all to propel him into his calling.

Putting It into Practice

Write: Record one way God has transformed your life since knowing Christ. Reflect on a season when God completely redirected your path, like Paul on the road to Damascus. Journal how that "interruption" changed your life's trajectory and how you've seen God's hand in it since. Write about any areas where you still resist His redirection, and invite Him to lead you fully.

Pray: Pray for a heart like Paul's: one that treasures Christ above all and sees every circumstance as an opportunity to glorify Him. Use Philippians 3:7-8 as your prayer: *"Whatever gain I had, I counted as loss for the sake of Christ."*

Act: Identify one fear, comfort, or personal ambition that might be holding you back from wholehearted obedience. This week, take a step to surrender it, whether that's initiating a gospel conversation, serving in a hard place, or embracing an uncomfortable call from God.

Study Philippians 4:11-13. Read different translations of the verse and study the original Greek for key words (I highly recommend the Blue Letter Bible resource). Ask God to teach you the secret of Philippians 4:11-13.

Practice gratitude even in hardship. Each day this week, list three things you can thank God for, especially in areas where you feel pressure, persecution, or weakness. Let 2 Corinthians 12:9 guide your heart: *"My grace is sufficient for you, for my power is made perfect in weakness."*

Like Paul writing letters to strengthen churches, reach out to someone who is discouraged in their faith. Share Scripture, pray for them, and remind them that the same God who sustained Paul through beatings, shipwrecks, and prison is their sustainer, too. It's easy to get focused on your own pain and suffering, but let your season of calamity propel you into more profound empathy for those around you.

Prayer for the Journey

Lord Jesus, thank You for the grace that saves and sends. Thank You for pulling me out of my old way of living and directing me towards You. Use my life—the good, the bad, and the ugly—to proclaim You, no matter the cost, to all who might hear of it. I don't want to stay hiding in the shadows, focused only on surviving my own trials and hardships. Lord, use my hardships! Use my pain and suffering! Mold me and mature me with those times of deepest pain. Grow my heart to be more loving and empathetic to the people around me. Help me not to be so focused on my own calamities that I forget to pour out Your love and Your Holy Spirit on the people I encounter. I surrender all of myself to You. Use me. No matter the cost. I choose You, Almighty God! In Jesus' name, Amen.

PART 3

Typical Responses to the Stories God Has Placed Us In

I sincerely hope that this time spent together studying the lives of seven significant men in the Bible and their Hero's Journeys has opened your eyes and your heart to the mighty hand of God in the midst of our own calamitous seasons. These are crucial examples of how God moves, works, and molds the lives and hearts of his saints. The Hero's Journey isn't some "educational" concept that should only be discussed in a classroom or amongst English Literature majors. No! Instead, The Hero's Journey is *God's story*, and we are taking it out of the secular, educational world and putting it back into the minds of those who love and serve our Heavenly Author. This story plotline is universally accepted as the greatest of all stories, suggesting it could only come from the Divine One Himself. Because we are made in His image, His story is written on every human heart.

It's easy to read about the lives of others who have walked The Hero's Journey and be inspired. It's a whole new ballgame when you're walking through the journey in *your own life*. If we all got a glimpse into the lives of Job, Abraham, Joseph, Moses, Joshua, David, and Paul *during* their times of testing, we probably wouldn't see strong, stable men with everything figured out. Instead, I'm sure we would see men in the midst of their deepest struggles, filled with doubts, confusion, fears, and a whole lot of tears. They were people just like you and me, and they didn't know the end of their stories. We have the privilege of learning how their stories end! But they were in the thick of things and had no idea what was around the next corner in their lives. They had to lean in *hard* to God's comfort and His divine will! We should start doing the same — even when it seems impossible. Shifting our perspective this way changes how we see both their struggles and our own.

    I remember a time shortly after my divorce had begun in 2020. I moved back in with my parents, whose property backed up to 250+ acres of timberland on a steep hillside. After receiving frustrating news from my ex-husband's attorney that made my blood boil in rage (to be honest, I can't even remember what exactly it was – just that I was immeasurably irate). I hopped in my 2005 Nissan Frontier pickup and zoomed up the old logging road at ridiculous speeds. I remember looking through my tears to see dust billowing behind me in the rearview mirror. The rage within me was directed at both my ex *and* the Lord. I finally made it high up on a little overlook on the hillside, where I got out of my truck, climbed into the truck bed (because I clearly wasn't high enough or close enough for God to hear me), and began screaming at the top of my lungs at the Lord. I poured out my anger as hot tears fell from my face. I remember asking God why he would let this happen to me. I remember reminding him of the countless hours I had spent begging the Lord to save my marriage. I remember the seething anger I felt towards God as I accused Him of abandoning me and my daughter to the fate of divorce. I remember feeling hatred towards God and feeling like He didn't protect my daughter or me during the marriage and in the divorce.

    Now, fast-forward to the time of this writing: it's August of 2025, five years later. I have repented for the many angry curses I slung towards the Lord in that season. I was never quite sure why the Lord allowed me to remember, with such vivid clarity, that particular evening on the side of that mountain. However, now that God has been revealing to me a fresh understanding of my own journey and the journeys of so many people in the Bible, I have finally learned why God allowed me to retain those painful, tear-stained memories: to share with you.

    When I went through my seasons of wilderness wandering and the refiner's fire, I certainly had my fair share of failures! I didn't learn any of this by floating through my trials (both literal and figurative) with sunshine and rainbows beaming from my smile, but through anger, tears, repentance, and surrender. I am not approaching these typical responses from a seat of judgment. I am explaining these as someone who has uttered *every single one* of these phrases and walked through each one of these places of heart-positioning with the Lord. I have known (and sometimes *still know*) the sting of anger towards the Lord. The difference now is that anger is followed by quick repentance and the surrender of my life (again) into the Potter's hands.

Your struggles, hardships, trials, heartbreaks, calamities, and wilderness seasons are all part of how God is molding you into the vessel of honor that he desires for you to be. We all wish that we could grow and be molded by God *without* hardships and pain, but God knows best! As we saw in the lives of King Saul and King Solomon, when The Hero's Journey is removed from an individual's life, all the wisdom in the world won't keep you from falling away from God's plan and purposes for your life.

As you read the following chapters, search your heart with honest openness. Do you see yourself in the same position? Do you hear your own voice uttering the same things? Do you feel the same anger and pain? In your past or in your present? Be vulnerable and honest with yourself. There is no judgment in these pages: only heartfelt camaraderie and a voice that says, "I've been there. I know. Now, let's walk through this together."

The times of testing and crushing are painful and difficult, yes, but the outcome is *always* worth it. The following few chapters are the most personal part of this book. Let's face it! Addressing our most difficult seasons of life with a perspective that says, "Hey, God's using this to grow and transform you!" isn't the easiest lesson to chew on. It'd be so much easier to say, "This is all so messed up and wrong! Why would God let this happen to you?!" But that way of thinking is missing the key understanding of the God who transforms us from glory to glory! He's the God who meets us where we are, *then* wants us to grow deeper and deeper in our relationship with Him. Our God is the Master Writer and Creator of perfect stories - even when they're the most complex stories we have ever walked through. When it doesn't make sense and you want to give up, lean into His arms, surrender control to Him, and trust the Author to write your story exactly how He desires it to be. Are you ready? Let's get started.

CHAPTER II

"Why is This Happening to Me?" The Pity-party Response

Remember when I told you that I struggled immensely with pride throughout high school, college, and my young adult years? That pride led me to ask this very question when my life started to turn upside down. Looking back now at my particular case, I believe God used The Hero's Journey to drastically transform my heart and save me from the more profound consequences of my sinful lifestyle choices. Although I am still dealing with some consequences from those sins, I shudder to think of all that I could be living in had God not intervened on my behalf. My pride—the belief that I was doing "everything right" when I was in fact doing everything *wrong*—was the very thing that led me to the Pity-Party Response.

"God, why are you letting this happen to me?!?!" I remember crying as my new marriage quickly unraveled into a nightmare. My perspective at the time was that God was removing blessings from my life. I had grown up believing that "Good things in life equaled God's blessing," while "Bad things in life meant God had removed blessing and favor." However, as we read and learned in the lives of Job, Abraham, Joseph, Moses, Joshua, David, and Paul, "good things" *does not mean* "blessed." Those men were some of the most profoundly blessed men in all of history, yet they endured tremendous pain, loss, waiting, and wilderness wanderings. That truth alone dismantles the shallow promises of "Prosperity Gospel" theology, doesn't it?

When my first marriage went south, I based my joy and identity on the state of my relationship. When things seemed good, I smiled with superficial joy, assuming things were finally on an uphill trajectory. This never lasted long. The abusive cycle would restart, and send me spiraling back into "God, why are you letting this happen to me?!?" In Chapter One, I told you about the point where I realized I had two choices before me: I would either become a shell of a person– miserable and living in constant fear – or throw myself at the feet of Jesus in absolute surrender. Thankfully, I chose surrender to Jesus.

I wish I could say everything started turning around at that point, but it didn't. What did change was my heart towards the Lord. Slowly, I began to move away from the self-pity response and started seeking God more earnestly. I developed a habit of waking up at 4:30 every morning to spend an hour and a half in prayer and intercession for my marriage. In those raw and tear-filled mornings, my faith became *real* for the first time. I wasn't living off the faith of my childhood anymore – I was cultivating an authentic, personal relationship with the Lord. God was using that wilderness season to strip away my pride and draw me close to His heart.

Maybe you can relate. Have you found yourself crying, "God, why are you letting this happen to me?" while swirling in a tornado of circumstances beyond your control? I can relate. At times, the voice that screams this question can be deafening in your mind. There were times I tried to pray to God and found myself ending up screaming this question at Him. That's the essence of the Pity Party: it's raw, emotional, and loud. Scripture reminds us of a sobering truth: "*The heart is deceitful above all things, and desperately wicked; who can understand it?*" I like how Eugene Peterson worded it in The Message: "*The heart is hopelessly dark and deceitful, a puzzle that no one can figure out*" (Jeremiah 17:9). Our genuine, raw emotions are not to be trusted. The self-pity we want so desperately to validate? It's a trap! Looking at The Hero's Journey through God's perspective exposes the Pity Party for what it is: selfish and flawed. Ouch. This is even hard for me to write! Because it's touching on my own heart most of all!

The Pity Party focuses entirely on our emotions, which we know cannot be trusted, and ignores the larger truth that God is shaping and growing us through hardship. It can *feel* comforting and appealing in the moment. However, the reality is, when you find yourself in the Pity Party mindset, it's like wrapping yourself in a blanket that's slowly catching fire. It might feel warm and cozy at first, but it ends up burning you. There are several significant flaws in the mindset behind the Pity Party that, if left unchecked, will slowly poison your mind and cripple your growth in the Lord.

Flaw #1: It Fixates on the Problem Instead of the Solution

A pity party dwells on *what's wrong* instead of seeking *what's next*. This reinforces a cycle of hopelessness rather than sparking faith-filled action. Paul reminds us in Philippians to focus on *"whatever is true,...honorable,... just,... pure,... lovely,... commendable, if there is any excellence,... worthy of praise, think about these things"* (Philippians 4:8, shortened). This powerful verse directly confronts the Pity Party mindset, calling us to shift our focus from despair to hope by setting our minds on God's truth—not the untrustworthy emotions of our flesh.

Flaw #2: It Centers On the Self Instead of On God

"Woe is me" thinking puts our own feelings, struggles, and injustices at the center of the story rather than God's sovereignty and presence in the midst of it. This mindset whispers, *"God is absent"* or *"God can't redeem this."* These lies are directly contrary to the truth that God tells us in Romans 8:28: *"And we know that for those who love God all things work together for good, for those who are called according to his purpose."* The Pity Party response isn't just unhealthy—it's in direct opposition to God's Word.

Flaw #3: It Magnifies Temporary Circumstances Over Eternal Perspective

Pity parties zoom in on present pain as if it were permanent, leaving joy and hope out of reach. However, Scripture calls us to *"fix our eyes not on what is seen, but on what is unseen"* (2 Corinthians 4:18), which really does shrink our current problems in light of eternity. Satan would love nothing more than for us to get so caught up in our own pain and perplexities that we forget to look towards our future and the will of God for our lives.

When we are overly focused on our problems, we can't maintain an eternal perspective on God's calling in our lives.

Flaw #4: It Isolates Rather Than Invites Community

A pity party often lulls us away from the very people who could encourage, pray for, and support us. This is a dangerous place to be— especially in the midst of a trial! *Proverbs 18:1* warns that *"Whoever isolates himself seeks his own desire; he breaks out against all sound judgment."* Isolation leads to poor judgment! Additionally, Galatians 6:2 calls us to bear one another's burdens! God places people in our lives for strength and accountability, but Pity Parties cut us off from the lifeline of community.

Flaw #5: It Shuts Out Gratitude and Worship

This may be the most dangerous flaw of all in the Pity Party mindset. When we enter into this mindset, the first things to leave are gratitude and worship. Gratitude and worship are oxygen to the soul in times of trial; pity parties close the window to both. Paul reminds us to *"Rejoice always, pray without ceasing, give thanks in **all** circumstances; for this is the will of God in Christ Jesus for you"* (1 Thessalonians 5:16-18). We don't give thanks and worship God because the pain is good, but because *God is good in the midst of it.*

As you know, my own story didn't end with a joyful reunion. It ended in abuse and a painful divorce. Not the ending I was hoping for, begging for, or praying for. I was wrecked and broken. As the divorce began and my ex started his slandering campaign—in the church I was attending at the time, amongst family and friends, and in the courtroom—the Pity Party response kept raising its ugly head again in me! I found myself spiraling into some of the same mentalities I had begun to walk away from! In addition to the Pity Party, I found myself saying: "This isn't fair!"

Which leads us to our next response.

CHAPTER 12

"I'm a Good Person; This Shouldn't be Happening to Me!" The THAT'S-NOT-FAIR Response

In April of 2020, amidst COVID lockdowns, I sat in my living room with my parents, a family friend, and my then-husband. I explained to him that I would be leaving him because of the threats he made toward me and my daughter, the deep sense of unsafety in our home, and the host of broken wedding vows. He cried and begged for another chance, but I had seen that charade too many times before. When I firmly refused him, I saw a visible shift come across his face. He had dropped the mask and revealed the unempathetic person underneath.

After I left, he wasted no time in launching his slander campaign. It was *hard* to walk through! Friends I had developed and sincerely trusted began to remove me from our social circles. The church I attended believed his word over mine. I was asked to step down from ministry positions. My heart was left feeling more broken than ever. Not only was my marriage broken, but now I was dealing with the shatter effect from the lies of an angry, controlling man.

And it wasn't fair—or so I thought. I remember crying out: "This is wrong! This is unjust! God, where are You in all of this? I've prayed, I've served, I've obeyed! Why is this happening to me?" I echoed this sentiment countless times over the following months. It just didn't make sense to me! My fear of the unknown mixed with rage at the injustice of my ex-husband's lies and the failures of the Family Court system all fueled the "That's Not Fair!!" echoing in my heart.

Especially when faced with the Family Court system, I found myself repeating these thoughts to the Lord: "God, this isn't fair! How is he getting away with this? How does his perjury go unpunished?" I found myself praying along with many of David's Psalms, like "*The boastful shall not stand before your eyes; you hate all evildoers. You destroy those who speak lies; the Lord abhors the bloodthirsty and deceitful man*" (Psalms 5:5–6), and "*I have done no wrong, yet they are ready to attack me. Arise to help me; look on my plight! O LORD God Almighty, the God of Israel, rouse yourself to punish [them]; show no mercy to wicked traitors*" (Psalm 59:4-5). Along with many other Psalms, I would angrily pray and declare these words in hopes that God would reach down into my circumstance and bring swift justice to the wrongs I was being dealt. But if I'm honest, I wasn't praying in submission to God's will. I was twisting His Word to demand *my* will. I wasn't asking for *His* justice. I was demanding He enforce *my* version of justice.

Many of us often point to Jesus' words in the Gospel of John: "*Whatever you ask in my name, this I will do, that the Father may be glorified in the Son. If you ask me anything in my name, I will do it*" (John 14:13-14). This verse has become the backbone of the "Name it, Claim it" theology, but Jesus' name is not a magic formula. This thinking misses the core of what Jesus was saying in this verse. What He meant was this: if we pray for anything that *brings glory to the Father's will*, He will do it. Essentially, prayers that really bring glory and honor to God come from a heart that is submitted to His will.

When I was praying these Psalms, I was *not praying in accordance with God's will*. Instead, I was trying to strong-arm God's Word to *my will*. When we fall into the "That's Not Fair" response to God's hand in our lives, we are trying to convince God to submit His will to ours. That's the essence of the "That's Not Fair" response: it assumes I know better than God. When I exalt my own sense of fairness over God's sovereignty, I commit idolatry. I enthrone my idea of justice above His wisdom.

It's like a marathon runner who stops mid-race, furious that another runner's lane looks smoother. Instead of pressing on, he argues with the officials, forgetting the real goal: the finish line. The rough stretches, hills, and potholes are part of the race, designed to test endurance and build character. Refusing to run because *"it isn't fair"* guarantees you'll *never* cross the finish line.

Likewise, when we cry *"That's not fair!"* we risk missing God's sovereign purposes and grace. We become crippled not by the circumstances themselves, but by the mindset that demands God bend to our will. In truth, the "That's Not Fair" response can be more spiritually damaging than the trial itself. Here are some of those major flaws:

Flaw #1: It Assumes We Deserve Good Based on Our Own Righteousness

This mindset is rooted in self-righteousness: *"I'm good, so I deserve good things."* However, scripture is clear that *"there is no one righteous, not even one"* (Romans 3:10). Our standing before God is based on His grace, not our merit. Believing that our "goodness" determines how God treats us, we subtly try to make a "trade" with God: *my good behavior in exchange for favorable circumstances.* This cheapens God's love for us from covenantal love to a mere transaction. This mindset also wrongly assumes that only pleasant circumstances are blessings. When things go well in our lives, we incorrectly think, "Oh, I'm so blessed! God's favor is upon me!" However, just because things are going well in life doesn't mean that we are blessed! Times of pruning and the Potter's crushing are a blessing too! To call them unfair is to accuse God of being unjust—and that borders on heresy! Let that sink in.

If you find yourself stuck in the "That's Not Fair" mindset when faced with God's pruning hand, remember this important truth: *the fruit of the hard seasons is much sweeter than the fruit of the "good" and easy times.*

Flaw #2: It Measures Fairness by Human Standards, Not God's Wisdom

What feels "fair" to us is often short-term comfort and entirely self-focused. What God calls good is eternal transformation. We can never fully understand why God does what He does. As God said through Isaiah: *"For my thoughts are not your thoughts, neither are your ways my ways, declares the LORD. For as the heavens are higher than the earth, so are my ways higher than your ways and my thoughts than your thoughts"* (Isaiah 55:8–9). Our Creator God is infinite and timeless, with wisdom and understanding beyond our comprehension. We are finite and limited! From our perspective, Job's suffering looked unfair! From God's vantage point, it revealed His glory and Job's refined faith (Job 42:5–6). Similarly, God works things in our own lives to reveal His glory and to refine our faith – even when we don't like or understand it.

Flaw #3: It Forgets the Example of Christ

If anyone could say, *"This isn't fair!"*, it was Jesus! Perfectly innocent and holy, He endured tremendous betrayals, severe beatings, and a horrible death of crucifixion. His story is the ultimate "That's not fair!!!" Yet, He *"entrusted Himself to Him who judges justly"* (1 Peter 2:23). He submitted to God's justice and plan. In Gethsemane, when His humanity begged for another way, He still submitted to the Father's will. This story-of-all-stories is the ultimate reminder that no unfairness we endure outweighs the mercy God has shown us in Christ.

Flaw #4: It Can Breed Bitterness Instead of Trust

Lastly, when we cling to "That's Not Fair," this mindset hardens the heart, making us view God as *withholding* rather than *faithful*. This thinking begins with the assumption that we know what's best. Then, when God doesn't align with our expectations, bitterness, anger, and mistrust take root. Hebrews 12:15 warns against a "root of bitterness" that corrupts many. Bitterness blinds us to God's sustaining presence during hardship! This is Satan's goal for us when we walk through The Hero's Journey in our own lives: bitterness towards God, but God's goal for the journey is to refine us and bring us closer to Him.

When the cry of "That's not fair!" goes unanswered in the way *we* want, it often boils over into anger at God. This is a dangerous turning point: instead of trusting His wisdom, we begin to resent Him. Many of us have prayed, served, and sacrificed, only to feel betrayed when hardship still came, leading to anger towards God, which is precisely where we turn next.

CHAPTER 13

"God, I'm Mad at You for Letting This Happen to Me! How Can I Trust You?" The Angry-At-God Response

Now, *this response* is a doozy. It's hard to talk about because it's so real, raw, and—in all honesty—repulsive. These were the ugliest tears I've cried: angry tears. When my life felt as though it were falling apart and there was no hope on the horizon, deep anger and resentment boiled up within me. That anger and resentment landed on a myriad of people in my life, but God was my primary target.

In April of 2023, my ex-husband took me back to Family Court again. At first, I entered the modification process with faith and courage, but all of that unraveled within me in December of that year. My ex was trying to take *everything* from me: sole, legal, and residential custody, a drastically different parenting schedule that favored him, and more. The modification hearing was a disaster. Witnesses lied on the stand, my attorney was useless, and halfway through, the judge forced me into an off-the-record settlement where I felt bullied, isolated, and coerced into agreements I never wanted. I even asked for my husband to be in the courtroom with me to discuss these things, and the judge refused! And then, just like that, it was all over, and the judge closed the modification hearing. I left feeling humiliated, betrayed, and furious—not just at the court system, but at God Himself.

When my husband and I got to the car, I unleashed a barrage of anger, curses, and screams towards the Lord. I felt so unjustly treated by the Family Court system, by my joke-of-an-attorney, and by God. "Where was God in all of this? How could He let this happen?! I had so much faith in Him, and this is how He betrays me?!" These thoughts bubbled in my heart like percolating coffee over a hot stove. I was *angry* at God.

A few months later, I discovered my ex's attorney had illegally filed paperwork without notifying me, making additional changes that were never discussed or agreed upon in court. I had already fired my attorney, and she took full advantage of that. The judge signed the paperwork without question. Another injustice. Another wave of fury. I couldn't understand why God was allowing me to walk through such blatant injustices! I remember shouting at God: *"Doesn't Your Word say You hate liars and false witnesses?! Then why are You letting them do this to me?!"* I filed paperwork to have the faulty paperwork amended and corrected. After three months of waiting for the judge to sign the papers, he *denied my petition.* I was out of options. I was angry. I was broken. This was wrong, and I couldn't even begin to see past my red-hot rage.

I know I'm not the only one who's ever been angry at God (sarcasm noted). I learned an essential reality in the midst of my anger towards God: my rage didn't wound God; it *only poisoned my own heart towards God.* It clouded my vision, stole my peace, and blinded me to His presence. I lost sight of so many essential things in that year of unanswered questions. In hindsight, I can see how God was walking *with* me through it all—teaching, molding, pruning, and growing me. However, all I could see was the raw rage within me, and God took the brunt of my verbal assaults. Despite all the evil I said towards Him, God—in all of His goodness and faithfulness—never left me or abandoned me. Even when I snarled in disgust at His Words about injustice, He still loved me and waited patiently for me. He still held my broken heart in His hands.

What a good God we serve! Even when He is on the receiving end of our unbridled anger and vehement rage, He stays close to us. No one else could take the brunt of such an emotional assault and remain so good and faithful! It's important to note here that this is never a license to rage against God. Anger toward God is still sin, and it warps our view of who He is. The Lord wants to walk with us through those emotions, not to become the target of them. That's why we must examine the dangerous flaws in the "Angry-at-God" response and confront the lies it plants in our hearts about His character.

Flaw #1: It Assumes God Owes Us for Our Service

Just like I was angry towards God after a troublesome modification hearing because I "had such faith going into the hearing," this mindset treats obedience like a bargaining chip! "If I serve You, You owe me good things." Or "If I have faith in You in this, You should respond favorably towards me." The reality is this: God owes us nothing! Sometimes we too easily forget that we are *His* creation. Does He love us immensely? Yes. But is He still the God of the universes, Creator of all, and the perfect, holy, righteous King? Yes! Everything He gives is *by grace*, not earned wages. There is nothing we can do that even comes close to being deserving of payback from the King of kings, just like Paul says in Romans: *"Who has given a gift to him that he might be repaid?"* (Romans 11:35). The moment we start treating God like a cosmic vending machine, we've replaced love with transaction and surrendered trust for entitlement.

Isaiah drives this home with a gut-punch: *"...All our righteous deeds are like a polluted garment. We all fade like a leaf, and our iniquities, like the wind, take us away"* (Isaiah 64:6). According to the Blue Letter Bible, that Hebrew word in Isaiah for "polluted garments" is *ida* (pronounced "ih-dah"), which literally means "menstrual rags." Gross. And, what's more? This is the only time in the Bible that this word is used: when referring to our righteous deeds. No matter how "good" we think we are, those "good deeds" don't even come close to being clean underpants for God! They are worn, bloody, and disgusting! How foolish to think we can leverage our "good deeds" into a divine payback. When we do, we are demanding that God bow to our will rather than surrendering to His.

Flaw #2: It Ignores the Truth About God's Character

Anger toward God assumes He has unfairly wronged us, which is a direct accusation of His character. Regardless of the circumstances we face, God is *"...righteous in all his ways and kind in all his works"* (Psalm 145:17). Did you catch that? In *all of His ways*. Even when we don't understand His methods, He is still righteous and perfect. It is not our place to judge

God! We do not sit on His holy throne! **He alone sits on the throne and judgment seat.** And, again, we have to remember this truth: His plans are for our ultimate good, even if they're painful now (Romans 8:28). When we choose to judge the Lord and respond to Him in anger, that mindset warps our view of God into a cosmic villain rather than a loving Father. Satan loves for us to see God this way, because that's precisely how Satan views God.

Flaw #3: It Elevates Our Judgment Above God's

When we persist in the "Angry-at-God" response, what we're really saying is, *"If I were God, I'd do this better."* That is frightening arrogance. This assumes that we—*mere, finite mortals*—would be better at God's job than He is. God Himself addresses this mindset when speaking to Job in Job 38-42! God asks Job questions like,

> *"Where were you when I laid the foundation of the earth?... Have you commanded the morning since your days began, and caused the dawn to know its place?... Have the gates of death been revealed to you, or have you seen the gates of deep darkness? Have you comprehended the expanse of the earth?... Will you even put me in the wrong? Will you condemn me that you may be in the right? Have you an arm like God, and can you thunder with a voice like his?"*

The Lord thunders these questions not because He's cruel, but because He is infinitely wise. We are not. Whenever you feel yourself falling into the "Angry-at-God" response, read Job 38-42 for a positive perspective on the greatness and goodness of our God!

Anger is a real emotion. Whenever you feel that rising inside of you towards the Lord, remind yourself of this truth from God: *"For my thoughts are not your thoughts, neither are your ways my ways, declares the* L<small>ORD</small>*. For as the heavens are higher than the earth, so are my ways higher than your ways and my thoughts than your thoughts"* (Isaiah 55:8-9). God's wisdom is infinitely higher than ours. There's no question or doubt about that. Anger at God almost always has pride sitting in the passenger seat, whispering lies to us that say we know better than God. Check your heart when anger enters! Pride is probably close beside it. And pride makes us the judge of God, rather than letting God be the judge of all. This was Lucifer's sin that got him cast out of Heaven and into eternal damnation.

Flaw #4: It Forgets That Trials Are Part of the Christian Life

This is the heartbeat of this entire book: **trials are part of growing up in our faith.** The "I've done so much for You, so You owe me!" mindset expects a life free from hardship as a reward for service. This is simply not God's design. In fact, it's actually the *opposite*! Jesus promised His followers trouble in this world (John 16:33). Paul also taught that suffering is part of the Christian lifestyle: *"We are afflicted in every way, but not crushed; perplexed, but not driven to despair; persecuted, but not forsaken; struck down, but not destroyed"* (2 Corinthians 4:8). This is further compounded in Romans, which says, *"we suffer with him so that we may also be glorified with him."* (Romans 8:17). In Western culture especially, we resist the idea that following Jesus involves suffering. However, if we reject this vital aspect of our growth as disciples of Christ, we stunt our development and bind ourselves to being infant Christians. This mindset eventually sets us up for disillusionment and bitterness when hardship inevitably comes.

Flaw #5: It Undermines Trust and Relationship with God

Perhaps the most dangerous effect of anger at God is that it allows temporary pain to dictate whether He is trustworthy. **Our temporary circumstances do not dictate God's character.** The God of creation—perfect and unchanging since the dawn of time—is not changed simply because of our temporary struggles. To believe the opposite is downright *false*. Instead, we are called to trust the Lord, even when everything might be falling apart around us (remember Job and Joseph?). The prophet Habakkuk words it beautifully in a prayer he wrote: *"Though the fig tree should not blossom, nor fruit be on the vines, the produce of the olive fail and the fields yield no food, the flock be cut off from the fold and there be no herd in the stalls, yet I will rejoice in the* LORD*; I will take joy in the God of my salvation"* (Habakkuk 3:17–18). This is the type of prayer we could all write down, put on the dashboard of the car, or pin it on the mirror above the bathroom sink. This prayer is the posture of trust: "Even if I lose everything, I will still worship You. Like Habukkuk, I will still rejoice in You. Like James, I will count it all joy! For I know that *You are good in all of Your ways!*" Faith trusts God's heart even when His hand and His ways are hard to understand! Responding in anger to God in our most challenging seasons is like splashing frigid water on someone freezing to death. And guess what? You're the one freezing to death, having distanced yourself from the warmth of God's comfort and safety.

God shapes us through our trials into the image of Christ. The hands of our perfect Potter are constantly working to crush, squash, squeeze, and mold us into the person He wants us to be: like Jesus! A lump of clay never spins on the wheel just to protest to every press and push of the potter's hands: "You're ruining me! How dare you!? Is that what you're really going to use me for? Why would you do that?! Just step aside, and let me mold myself!" That would be downright silly. Why? Because the clay has no vision of the beautiful, purposeful vessel it's becoming in the hands of the potter! Instead, the clay only feels the pressure. God responds to those angry whines like this: *"Who are you, O man, to answer back to God? Will what is molded say to its molder, 'Why have you made me like this?' Has the potter no right over the clay, to make out of the same lump one vessel for honorable use and another for dishonorable use?"* (Romans 9:20-21). His design is always perfect, even when His pressure feels unbearable. To rage against the Potter is to deny the very hands that are lovingly shaping us into Christ's image.

Don't let that ugly anger rise and overcome your heart towards the Lord. It will only harden your heart towards God and make you resistant to His comfort, love, wisdom, guidance, and plan for your life. It only cripples *you*. And if you, like me, have found yourself stuck in anger towards God, it's time for some humble repentance.

CHAPTER 14

"I Deserve This for All the Sins I've Committed."
The Woe-Is-Me, God's-Punishing-Me response

For me, this response showed up during one of the darkest valleys of my life. After three years of trauma, I was wrestling with complex PTSD, depression, and the crushing weight of divorce proceedings with my daughter's future hanging in the balance. Panic and anxiety triggers paired with relentless regret left me questioning everything I was doing. I lived with deep sadness over the last decade of my life. I sank into feeling convinced that every hardship was God's punishment for my failures. I would whisper to myself, *"This is what I deserve. For my sins. For my decisions. God is punishing me."* That belief left me hopelessly withdrawn, trapped in flawed theology.

I didn't land here overnight. I spiraled through the Pity Party mindset, stumbled into the "That's Not Fair!" response, and finally collapsed into the pit of *"Woe is me"* for some time. I remember feeling so lost and unsure of where to turn. I felt distant from God as I spiraled into myself. When you find yourself in this response to God, it can make you feel incredibly hopeless as the walls of your own circumstances and regret close in around you. As tempting as it can be (trust me, I know) to give up and give in to the dark emotions that surround the "God's Punishing Me" response, I want to shed some light on the truth of the matter: this way of thinking and responding to God's wilderness season also has some serious flaws in thinking and theology.

Flaw #1: It Misunderstands God's Character

First and foremost, the major flaw in this mindset is the view of God. It paints God primarily as a harsh punisher rather than a loving Father. This mindset warps His character and overlooks the truth of Scripture: *"There is now no condemnation for those who are in Christ Jesus"* (Romans 8:1). His discipline is restorative, not vindictive! We see this truth in Hebrews as well: *"For the Lord disciplines the one he loves, and chastises every son whom he receives"* (Hebrews 12:6). Viewing every hardship as punishment distorts our view of His heart toward His children and robs us of seeing His mercy in our trials. I would also add that distorting God's character in this manner also replaces the God of Creation—perfect and holy blended with love and mercy—with a god of our own creation.

Flaw #2: It Reduces Suffering to a Transactional Cause-and-Effect

This response treats all pain as payback for sin, as though life with God runs on a cosmic vending machine. We know that God's pruning hand actually sets us on The Hero's Journey to mature and transform us! That journey, although difficult, is filled with purpose and hope – not filled with judgment and condemnation. The "God's punishing me" response is a direct contrast to the character of God. Yes, there are instances in the Bible when God does punish his chosen people through exile, famine, drought, and slavery. That demonstrates part of God's character – perfect and holy – and is before Christ's sacrifice on the cross that restored unity between God and His creation. Now, when he is walking a child through The Hero's Journey, it is never out of punishment or judgment. The mindset that gets us stuck thinking this way assumes that all suffering is a direct result of personal sin! However, the Bible repeatedly challenges this way of thinking when the Lord's hand is at work in the transformation of one of His children. We see this in the lives of the men whom we have studied! Life in a fallen world includes suffering for many reasons: spiritual growth, refining faith, testing endurance, or revealing God's glory — not God's repayment for wrongdoing.

Flaw #3: It Forgets the Gospel

One of the most important things we need to keep in the forefront of our minds when facing the temptation of the "God's Punishing Me" mindset is that it directly contradicts the beauty of the Cross. The punishment for sin was fully poured out on Jesus at the cross (Isaiah 53:5–6; 2 Corinthians 5:21). To believe God is "getting back at us" is to imply Christ's sacrifice was insufficient – that your sin is somehow bigger than His blood can manage. Oofta. When you put it that way, the "God's Punishing Me" response is more than flawed thinking; it's an assault on the heart of the Gospel.

I can tell you from personal experience that, when you have a broken relationship with the Lord, *it's not His fault.* We are *always* the perpetrators of brokenness between our Heavenly Father and our own hearts. Remember that parable of the Prodigal Son? It wasn't the Father who pushed his son away; instead, the son chose to leave and live his own life. As soon as the son's heart changed towards the father, however, the father was quick to run to his son, embrace him, and restore the relationship.

When we are caught in the "God's Punishing Me" mindset, we cripple ourselves by our own decisions. It's not God's doing or His hand of punishment upon our lives! We know that *"God chose to give up His only son, so anyone who believes in Him would not perish but have everlasting life"* (John 3:16). Believers must remember: our suffering is not payment for sin – it's a tool for sanctification.

Flaw #4: It Breeds Hopelessness Instead of Faith

A long time ago, I remembered hearing someone tell me an important truth about guilt and shame. They said that guilt comes from the Holy Spirit to bring conviction and correct *behavior.* Shame, on the other hand, comes from the enemy to *attack your identity,* to whisper lies in your ear about how terrible *you* are. This is a massive piece of the "God's Punishing Me" mindset: **guilt versus shame.** When we confuse the two, shame paralyzes us and drives us away from God instead of toward repentance and hope in Him. That's why Paul says the Spirit's work leads to life and freedom (Romans 8:2), not despair. The Holy Spirit will point out our sins with a holy guilt that leads us to repentance and deeper communion with the Lord. That is the KEY! When you start to feel conviction over something, check yourself: are you feeling the movement towards repentance? Or are you feeling like *you yourself* are worthless? If your hardship makes you think, *"I'm worthless, God hates me,"* you can be sure that's the enemy, not the Spirit.

Flaw #5: It Misses the Opportunity for Growth

This mindset wastes the very trials God desired to use for our growth and transformation. It actually stumps our growth and makes the pain we are experiencing seem *worthless* due to our own choices! That is *not* what God wants for us! He is not a vindictive God who just wants to inflict pain like a bully on a playground. That is directly contrary to the very nature and character of our God! If trials are seen only as punishment, we end up resisting the Spirit's deeper work in us through them (James 1:2–4). This short-circuits the very transformation God aims to produce and renders our pain null and void. We cheapen our own pain and trials with this mindset.

I want you to imagine a good King in a faraway land. This attentive king declared an edict across his land that would help his kingdom grow stronger and more fruitful, although the initial changes would be more complex for some of his subjects. One such subject had fallen on difficult times and was struggling with the new edict. The King asked a messenger to send the servant a message of encouragement along with necessary provisions for the season ahead. The messenger delivered a sealed letter from the King during this season of hardship. Inside, it says, *"This trial will strengthen you for the road ahead. I know it's hard. Remember, I am not against you — trust Me. I have supplied you with all that you need for this season."* But when the weary servant got the letter, he skimmed the words and only saw that it said, *"This is a trial. I am against you."* The servant, discouraged and feeling hopeless, walked away from the messenger with his head down, missing the guidance and rejecting the resources the King sent to help him overcome. This is very much how we respond to the wilderness season and times of testing that the Lord brings us through when we believe God is just punishing us. We read only certain parts of the Bible and interpret them through a skewed lens, walking away from the Messenger of the Holy Spirit and rejecting the resources God has given us to make the journey.

CHAPTER 15

"Why Do I Even Try?" The Apathetic Response

If one animal could embody the idea of apathy, it would be the ostrich. Contrary to myth, ostriches don't bury their heads in the sand; they flop down, stretch out their necks, and blend in, hoping danger passes them by. That's what apathy does: *"I'll just wait this out. I won't fight. I won't care. I'll hide until it's over."* Now, don't get me wrong. I still wouldn't encourage anyone to approach an ostrich in the wild! They'll likely not be so unassuming for a human. However, when a dangerous predator is near, ostriches will choose the apathy route! Apathy, according to Webster's dictionary, is the lack of feeling, emotion, interest, or concern. It is compared to words such as "impassiveness" and " indifference." Like that ostrich, apathy is the decision to disengage, give up, or stop caring.

Apathy can be the deadliest poison of all these flawed responses to the Potter's molding. And here's a critical truth behind apathy: Apathy is rebellion in disguise. Spiritual apathy doesn't always *look* like rebellion!

Apathy is sneaky and subtle—a slow-working poison. It lives and acts as a chameleon. Sometimes it looks like sitting down and waiting for life to "just pass over us." Other times, it can even come across as "hyper-spiritual," as when someone says, "The Lord's plan will work itself out!" Or "If God wants this to happen, He's going to make it work out!" Sometimes, it can come across as depression, distractions, or even laziness. Regardless of how apathy looks in your situation, it will always end up leaving you vulnerable to Satan's attacks. It will leave the gates of your heart and your faith unguarded. And the worst part? When we engage with and remain in apathy, it steals your chance to stand firm in your faith, to fight for what matters, and to watch God's hand at work in the very trial we wished away!

Scripture pulls no punches when addressing apathy. It often appears under the Biblical terms such as lukewarmness, slothfulness, spiritual sleep, and neglect of duty. This is most clearly seen in John's revelation, when Jesus said to the church of Laodicea: *"I know your works: you are neither cold nor hot. Would that you were either cold or hot! So, because you are lukewarm… I will spit you out of my mouth"* (Revelation 3:15-16). Jesus warns the church in Laodicea that spiritual halfheartedness (which is apathy!) is repulsive to Him, and He calls for repentance and renewed zeal in the face of apathy. The alternative is being spat out of God's mouth. That's a scary place to be!

As you can see, there are significant flaws in this dangerous mindset that can trap you. If you feel yourself slipping into this response, don't panic – but don't delay either. Apathy is subtle, but it is deadly. And the good news is that Jesus never leaves us in it without a way of escape. Let's look at the flaws of this mindset so you can identify them and fight back before apathy strangles your faith.

Flaw #1: It Rejects God's Purpose in the Trial

Throughout this book, we've seen how God uses trials as His refining fire. Hardship is not random – it's purposeful. When we "check out" spiritually, we refuse to engage with the refining, strengthening, and maturing work God intends to do in the hardship. James reminds us plainly to *"Count it all joy, my brothers, when you meet trials of various kinds, for you know that the testing of your faith produces steadfastness.… that you may be perfect and complete, lacking in nothing"* (James 1:2-4). This has been one of the key verses of this whole book! When we approach the trials of our lives with a Godly perspective, we will come to know that the trials are *training grounds* for perseverance and character, as we see in James 1:2-4 and additionally in Romans 5:3-5. Stepping away from engagement in the journey (apathy) is like walking out of the gym halfway through a workout or quitting halfway through a marathon! We reject the very growth, purposes, and victory that God designed for us.

Flaw #2: It Substitutes Survival for Godly Stewardship

It's easy to be faithful when life feels easy. But authentic discipleship calls for faithfulness in *every* season. Paul expresses this when he tells God's servants, *"It is required of stewards that they be found faithful"* (1 Corinthians 4:2). God *requires* us to be faithful stewards! Not just to get by one day at a time and "just survive." Remember the definition of apathy: the lack of feeling, emotion, interest, or concern. When applied to God's will for your life, an apathetic response means we lack feeling, interest, or regard for God's will in our lives. Yikes. That's a scary place to be.

Jesus confronts this head-on in the parable of the talents (Matthew 25:24–30). Jesus, when explaining this parable, says this:

> *"He who had received the one talent came forward, saying, 'Master,... I was afraid, so I hid your talent in the ground. Here, you have what is yours.' But his master answered him, 'You wicked and slothful servant!... Cast the worthless servant into the outer darkness. In that place there will be weeping and gnashing of teeth" (Matthew 25:24-30).*

An apathetic servant who hides his talents is cast out and seen as worthless—similar to what Jesus says to the church of Laodicea in Revelation. The same can be said of passivity in the face of hardship. It is essentially taking the investment that God has entrusted to us and burying it in the ground, much like that ostrich. Instead of multiplying what we've been given, we're hiding it in the ground until conditions improve and "feel better." God doesn't call us to hide; He calls us to invest.

Flaw #3: It Opens the Door for Spiritual Rot

When we sit back and do nothing in the midst of the hardest seasons of our lives, our hearts, spirits, and minds are being slowly drained of strength. To remain strong throughout the journey, we must, like David, *"strengthen [ourselves] in the LORD [our] God"* (1 Samuel 30:6, emphasis *added*). There is no neutral here! Apathy drains you. When hardships come, God designs those trials to help us specifically look to *Him* for sustenance, guidance, strength, wisdom, and perseverance. **That's the antidote to apathy: leaning into God's presence, promises, and power.** If we don't, our faith muscles shrivel. Unchecked apathy leads to spiritual atrophy. Our hearts grow cold, leading us to fall away from God. Hebrews warns us, *"**Take care**… that none of you may be hardened by the deceitfulness of sin"* (Hebrews 3:12–13). This is the ultimate WASTE of the trials in your life. Ignoring God in trials doesn't put us on pause; it puts us in reverse! The danger of apathy is that this movement away from God's voice often takes place *without us even realizing it.*

Flaw #4: It Forgets that God's Kingdom Advances in Every Season

One of the hardest consequences of divorce is having your kids miss out on special occasions, family get-togethers, and holiday celebrations. My sweet daughter, who is six years old at the time of this writing, is getting old enough now to recognize that she doesn't get to make it to all of our family events. She missed the 4th of July this year because she was with her dad. When she got home after that weekend, she found out that we had a large family party while she was gone. She was so distraught that we celebrated "without her" and took it very personally. It was a hard conversation to explain to her little six-year-old brain: "Well, honey, even when you go to your dad's house, life continues here! We can't stop doing everything and wait for you to come home. We always try to plan things that include you, but sometimes that doesn't always work with your schedule." Her tear-stained face was so heartbreaking as she tried to understand the difficult concept.

The same concept applies to God and His Kingdom. The apathetic response to The Hero's Journey in our lives assumes that God will take "days off." The Kingdom of God will not be "paused" until we feel like life is stable again! His Kingdom is vibrant with life—*always* advancing—with or without our participation. That may feel uncomfortable, but it's reality.

Although it might feel easier to check out and stop trying when things get hard, God does His most powerful work in *our* weakest moments. Actually, He promises this to Paul: *"My grace is sufficient for you, for my power is made perfect in weakness"* (2 Corinthians 12:9). Checking out during the trials means missing the opportunity to see Him display His strength in our weakness.

Flaw #5: It Denies the Call to Persevere and Bear Witness

The Christian life is a race that demands perseverance. The New Testament is filled with calls to "stand firm," "endure," and "run with perseverance." We see this in Hebrews 12:1–2, *"...Let us also lay aside every weight, and sin which clings so closely, and let us run with endurance the race that is set before us, looking to Jesus, the founder and perfecter of our faith,"* and in Galatians 6:9, *"...Let us not grow weary of doing good, for in due season we will reap, if we do not give up."* When we persevere in hardship, our very endurance becomes a testimony of God's sustaining power. Apathy, on the other hand, silences that testimony. When we choose apathy, our testimony becomes that of the disobedient servant with the one talent and says, "God isn't worth trusting in the storm." That's a lie, and Satan loves it.

Imagine this scenario: A strong fortress with thick, high walls sat on an ideal hill, with a perfect view of any approaching enemies for miles around in every direction. One day, enemies had been sighted on the distant horizon. Because of the powerful walls and the mighty watchmen on their perches, the people inside the city were calm and felt secure. Days later, after the enemies had been seen, one watchman, on the most important and tallest watchtower, leaned on his spear. When the enemy had first been spotted, he kept his eyes on the horizon, scanning for movement, listening for the sound of approaching feet. As the days passed, the enemy hadn't been seen again. One day, the sun was warm, the wind gentle, and the waiting was long. This particular watchman, who held a key position in alerting the city, eventually sat down. "If danger comes, we'll deal with it then," he thought. His eyelids grew heavy. Before long, his head drooped, and the watchman fell fast asleep. As night fell, the sneaky enemy finally arrived, without warning, in the city. They traversed the valley below the city with great speed and determination. When they reached the city, they didn't have to attack with swords. They were shocked to arrive in a quiet, unprotected city. There was no bustling on the walls or calls from the watchmen. The enemy simply walked through an open gate, wide-eyed. No one had closed it? No one had sounded the alarm? They entered the city without a fuss or any defenses. They overtook the city and enslaved the people all because the key watchmen chose apathy. The danger wasn't in the strength of the enemy's attack; it was in the watchman's decision to check out.

CHAPTER 16

"Not today, Satan!" The "Hard-Things-Only-Come-From-Satan" Response

This is one of the most common responses I've seen among Christians when the Potter's hands press hard. Many people today prefer to view God as benevolent, peaceful, sunshine, and rainbows, like your average hippy at the Saturday Market in Eugene, Oregon, peddling crystals and "good vibes." That's a caricature of God, watered down into a "cosmic therapist" whose main job is to soothe, affirm, and comfort – never to confront, prune, or refine.

Western culture has come to an emotional state that prizes emotional safety and affirmation. Love is often defined as unconditional acceptance and support of lifestyles without challenge. Kindness often means to never acknowledge sin for what it is. Peace has been twisted to equate absolutely no conflict—unless someone dares to disagree, then the claws come out. Tragically, this distorted view of virtue has crept into the church, shaping our view of God Himself. The result? A soft, man-made "god" who never says "no," never disciplines, never demands, and never stretches His children. That's not the God of Scripture, the King who reigns in holy justice.

Additionally, many modern preachers, worship songs, and devotionals emphasize God's grace and compassion but omit passages on judgment, pruning, growth, transformation, and His blazing holiness—and they most certainly don't include the book of Job! This selective presentation leads to a stunted gospel: We hear "Come as you are," but not "Go and sin no more." We sing about His mercy, but rarely about His majesty and consuming fire (Hebrews 12:29). Over time, Christians raised in this environment can start to think of God *only* as a kind friend, while Satan is credited with all that feels uncomfortable. But here's the dangerous truth: when we believe this, we've elevated Satan's hand above God's sovereignty.

A god who is *only* viewed as kind and loving becomes a smaller, softer, man-made parody of the real God of Scripture. This god makes few demands, never confronts sin, and primarily exists to make our lives easier. We've fashioned a false god in our own image. True worship and submission to the Lord must hold both God's love *and* His holiness together. Only when we understand and include *both* of these aspects of God do we genuinely see His grace for what it truly is: the mercy of a holy God who chose to save undeserving sinners at the highest cost to Himself personally.

The God of Job, Abraham, Joseph, Moses, David, and Paul is not a soft, spineless caricature. He is holy, righteous, and just. And, yes! God allows for painful, devastating seasons to come upon His servants to grow and prepare them to best suit His purposes for their lives! And sometimes God will even release Satan to do this (as in Job's and Paul's cases). This is not an easy thing to talk about in the church today, because it so strongly challenges a HUGE swath of people's theologies about God. Well, call me a window cleaner, because I am about to scrub some theology away that's been clouding your view of the Lord and His mighty hand upon your life – even in the ugly times! Which means if we fight every hard season with a reflexive "Not today, Satan!" we may actually be resisting God Himself. Let's clear the fog. Let's scrub down this cloudy theology and take a hard look at the flaws:

Flaw #1: It Misdiagnoses the Source of Hardship

Not every trial is a demonic attack. Not every hardship is Satan trying to "take you out." Not every sickness is the devil (I bet that just ruffled some feathers!). Not all job losses, broken relationships, betrayals—you name the hardship—is an attack from the enemy. Many of these very things that we find ourselves warring *against* are actually allowed or ordained by God for refinement, testing, or discipline. God repeatedly reveals this brutal truth in His Word. We see this in Job's loss, Joseph's imprisonment, Paul's thorn, and countless others in the Bible. God's perfectly crafted authorship—not Satan's sabotage. If we assume all hardship is satanic, we can end up rebuking what God is actually using for our good. We war against the very thing God is trying to use to refine us, and we sabotage our own growth.

Flaw #2: It Resists God's Refining Work

This echoes the last point nicely. When God has appointed a specific Hero's Journey in the life of an individual—to teach endurance, deepen faith, or correct our path—and our first response is to "pray it away," we miss the maturity and fruit that God intended for that trial. James 1:2-4 reminds us that trials are meant to produce steadfastness that leads to maturity. The "Not Today, Satan" response steals the transformative power of the journey from us, wastes the pain in the hardship, and nullifies God's design to take us from one glory to another. We end up crediting Satan for God's perfect design. When the hardships come, instead of jumping to warfare prayers, our prayer should look like this: "Lord, open my eyes and my heart to Your will. Is this trial a learning moment designed for my growth? Or is this something You want me to partner with You in prayer against the enemy?"

Flaw #3: It Oversimplifies Spiritual Warfare

Yes, Satan really opposes God's people. We see this throughout the Bible, and most poignantly in the life of Jesus. However, spiritual warfare is not just praying or warring *against* something. That's only half of the element of battle: it's only playing defense. When we only see spiritual warfare as *REactive* to Satan, it's like tying one hand behind our backs. Spiritual warfare is also *PROactive* faith, holiness, and obedience. Revelation 12:11—*"And they have conquered him by the blood of the Lamb and by the word of their testimony, for they loved not their lives even unto death"*— shows that victory isn't always escaping the trial but enduring through it with testimony intact. Sometimes the greatest act of warfare is not what we rebuke but what we endure with faith.

Flaw #4: It Reduces Jesus' Name to a Quick Fix

When I was a little kid, I remember learning about the power of Jesus' name. One day, while outside immersed in some fort I was building out of blackberry briars, a yellow jacket began pestering me and my dog! No matter how much I swatted or shooed it away, it kept buzzing around me and in my ears. I was annoyed and a little freaked out. I remember yelling at that darn yellow jacket to "Go away in Jesus' name!" over and over... It didn't listen. I was using Jesus' name as a "magic charm" to get rid of a very regular pest.

Invoking "in Jesus' name" is not a magic phrase to make problems vanish. Jesus' name is the most potent, awe-inspiring name in the history of creation! Not some quick fix to get rid of a pest of the demonic or insect variety. Too many Christians treat John 14:13–14 ("*ask anything in My name, and I will do it*") as a blank check to claim whatever they want. That's not what Jesus meant. This is called the "Name it, Claim it" theology in Christianity. However, Biblically speaking, praying in Jesus' name means praying *according to His will and character*. We don't get to use Jesus' name for just anything and expect Him to respond like some magic genie in a bottle. Even Jesus Himself prayed, "*Not my will, but Yours be done*" (Luke 22:42). If God has willed that your hardship refine you, no amount of "I rebuke this in Jesus' name" will cancel it. Instead, the prayer of faith must also include submission to His will and His design for your life, just like Jesus prayed.

Flaw #5: It Creates Disillusionment with God

Lastly—and this point is so important—if we find ourselves believing "If I pray hard enough in Jesus' name, this trouble will go away," we set ourselves up for crushing disappointment when there is no movement in the direction we desire. Over time, that can erode trust in God's goodness and cause spiritual discouragement. God didn't fail. Rather, our theology was wrong. This will only breed bitterness and resentment towards God, sinking yourself into the depths of despair in the middle of your trial when you need God *the most*. All because we started with a flawed theology that "Anything bad comes from Satan."

To avoid this dangerous and overly common theology towards The Hero's Journey, we must have a balanced perspective. We do need to understand that we have a very real enemy who hates us and wants to destroy us. Yes, sometimes, God does want us to *"stand against the schemes of the devil"* and to wrestle *"against the rulers, against the authorities, against the cosmic powers over this present darkness, against the spiritual forces of evil in the heavenly places"* (Ephesians 6:11-12). That is a very real element of our faith and walking with the Lord. Additionally, there are times when hardships result from human sin and living in a broken world. But there is also this last reason: sometimes hardships come directly from God's loving discipline and desire to see us grow and transform. The wise believer always knows to test the situation Biblically, surrender it to the Lord, seek His will and direction in fervent prayer, and ask for wisdom and direction from the Lord—all before deciding whether to resist the hardship or submit to it.

PART 3 REFLECTION
When God's Path Gets Hard

Now, I'm sure that there are other responses to Potter's hands on your life. These are simply the ones I have known most personally and believe are a common for many believers, too. Each of these is a key starting point for you to identify where you land emotionally when calamities come knocking. This is where the journey shifts from theory to practice.

Now, it's time to do the hard work: self-assessment. Where do you truly stand among these responses? Which one do you tend to fall into when life presses in on you? On the following few pages, I encourage you—and pray for you, dear reader—to enter into a time of intimacy with the Lord. Surrender your heart and your pride to Him. Allow His Spirit to search the hidden corners of your soul, and invite His heavenly scalpel to cut away any flawed theology or mindsets that have been poisoning your relationship with Him. This is where the real work happens.

Take your time in this next section. Move slowly. Sit with each question and reflect honestly. Ask the Lord for His divine guidance and divine revelation, as James says, *"If any of you lacks wisdom, let him ask God, who gives generously to all without reproach, and it will be given him. But let him ask in faith, with no doubting..."* (James 1:5-6a). Don't rush through—because these moments of reflection may be the very tools and wisdom He uses to redirect your heart and restore your hope. And always remember this important truth: **God's most complex paths are not detours; they are the training ground for the soul**. The rugged wilderness is not wasted space, but sacred ground where He prepares the soul He is shaping for eternity. Let's follow the lead of our Great Potter, and let the soul-shaping begin.

Pause on the Path

Something my mom always told me regarding any relationship – whether friend, family, or romantic – was this: "It's not a matter of *if* there will be conflict, but *when* there will be conflict." The same principle can be applied to life as a whole. It's not a matter of *if* you will encounter trials, but *when* you will encounter trials.

When those hardships hit, please remember this: suffering in the Christian life is not an accident; it is a part of God's sovereign plan to form Christ in us and transform us more into the image of Christ (Romans 8:29). Unfortunately, our stubborn, human hearts often default to unhealthy responses: wallowing in self-pity, demanding "fairness," assuming God is punishing us, checking out in apathy, or blaming Satan for every challenge. However, Scripture calls us to something higher – to a deeper trust in Him and to see trials, not as interruptions, but as invitations into God's refining work.

Each step of the journey, even the hardest uphill climbs or when the wilderness feels endless, is carefully designed by the One who loves us enough to shape us for *eternity*. If we trust His hand, we can endure His training. If we lean on His Spirit, we can rejoice in His nearness. If we fix our eyes on Jesus, we can keep walking forward, confident that even the darkest paths lead to greater light.

Putting It Into Practice

Write: Take 15 minutes to journal honestly about which of the flawed mindsets from this chapter most resonates with you right now: the *pity* *party*, the *"That's Not Fair"*, the *self-punishment, anger towards God, apathy*, or the *"only from Satan"* response. Write out what situations tend to trigger that reaction in you. What words do you find yourself speaking over yourself and your situation? These words can be verbal, written, *or even dark thoughts* you have kept inside you. Then, beside each one, write a Biblical truth or verse that directly corrects it. Lastly, add a short prayer that says, "Lord, I repent for believing and partnering with this lie. Show me Your truth in my flawed thinking."

Pray: Ask the Lord to reveal where your heart has been resisting His refining hand. Pray for a greater awareness of His holiness, sovereignty, and love so that you can accept even the hard seasons as part of His good and purposeful plan. Thank Him for being a Father who disciplines and leads you toward Christlikeness.

Act: Choose one practical step this week to replace your flawed response with a faithful one. This could mean memorizing a verse that speaks to God's sovereignty, sharing honestly with a trusted believer about your struggle, or intentionally thanking God in the middle of a hardship instead of resisting it. Practice this step the moment you feel the old mindset trying to take root.

When you feel the old mindset rising, whether it's "this isn't fair," "God must be punishing me," or any of the others, *pause.* Take a breath. Then speak truth over it. Say out loud: *"God is sovereign. He is working this for my good. I will trust His hand."* You can also write the Trail Marker Scriptures above on prominent places around your home or in your car, and pray them over yourself and your situation.

Choose a song or psalm that focuses on God's holiness and sovereignty – not just His comfort – and sing it during your trial. Worship shapes perspective! Just as Job responded with worship, begin practicing this life-giving habit in your own circumstances as well.

Reach out to someone else going through hardship and speak life into them — remind them that trials are not wasted and that God's refining hand is on them, too. In comforting others, you often find your own faith strengthened.

Prayer for the Journey

Father in Heaven, I repent to You right now for my flawed theology and mindsets and for making false accusations against Your character and virtue. Lord, forgive me! I confess that, when life gets hard, I am quick to question, complain, get angry, or retreat. Forgive me for the times I have misunderstood and rejected Your refining hand. Teach me to see trials as *Your* perfect, holy training ground, not as random accidents or unfair punishments. Fill me with endurance, humility, and trust. Lord, I choose to submit my mind, my will, my emotions, my spirit, my heart, and my life to Your will and Your ways. I believe they are perfect and holy – even when I don't understand them. Help me to reject the lies of the enemy and to cling to the truth of Your Word. May I walk forward with my eyes fixed on Jesus, who endured the cross for the joy set before Him. Guard me from falling into flawed theologies and mindsets again. Let this day, reading this chapter of this book, be a turning point in my life. In Jesus' name, Amen.

PART 4

Next Steps on the Journey

Ok, the hard work had been done: exposing and addressing the flawed mindsets and theologies that so easily take root in our hearts during seasons of trial. This is never easy work, and if you've made it this far, take a deep breath and thank the Lord for His grace to reveal, convict, and guide you. Now, the next step is to rebuild on a Biblically-based, firm foundation—not on the shaky sand of human reasoning, cultural clichés, or self-help mantras!

Here's the good news: *you are not a lost cause!* You are not disqualified if you find yourself drawn to those flawed mentalities we just discussed. Remember, every single one of the men we studied — Job, Abraham, Joseph, Moses, Joshua, David, Paul, and others in the Bible, too—all had moments of weakness, sin, fear, or flawed responses. They were, as we like to say, "hot messes" at different points in their journey. Yet, God never abandoned or gave up on them. He never tossed them aside as a lost cause. We have *all* responded to God with flawed thinking and self-centered mindsets. It's part of our human nature, and it's the reason why God takes us through The Hero's Journey: so He can work a new creation within each one of us.

It isn't always pretty! In fact, it's mostly pretty unpleasant and challenging, full of ugly crying and heartwrenching prayers. However, our goal shouldn't be to *avoid* the journey. The goal of the Christian life was never comfort; it was always transformation. The Potter's wheel and refining fire are not meant to destroy you but to make you more like Christ, with a submitted, trusting heart—no matter the circumstances.

So what now? Up to this point, we've laid the groundwork. We have traced the foundation of God's divine plotline. We have exposed the typical human responses to His molding hand and dismantled the flawed thinking behind each one. We've taken time to reflect inward and to ask hard questions of our own hearts. Now comes the turning point: to actively step into the Potter's process with humility and faith. This next stage is not about mere survival. It's about leaning into His Spirit and walking with perseverance. It's about cultivating the kind of faith that honors the Lord in the midst of the trial.

Let's move forward together toward becoming vessels that not only endure hardship but also grow in maturity and bear lasting fruit that reflects His glory. The Potter has more in store for you than just making it through — He intends to shape you into something eternal. The first and most important piece of God's divine plotline to study, reflect upon, and open your heart to is the Savior and Redeemer of every story: Jesus.

CHAPTER 17

Jesus: The Author and Finisher

> *"...looking unto Jesus, the author and finisher of our faith, who for the joy that was set before Him endured the cross, despising the shame, and has sat down at the right hand of the throne of God."* — Hebrews 12:2 (NKJV)

It would be a grave mistake to write this book without including the one whose story is the most powerful and profound, the one who is both the Author *and* the Hero: Jesus Christ. His story is the culmination of all the stories we have studied thus far, and his story is the culmination of your story as well. Each of our journeys is carefully crafted to point to Him above all else. This is why Paul says in Romans: *"For from Him and through Him and to Him are all things.* **To Him be glory forever***. Amen"* (Romans 11:36). God is crafting a testimony within each of our stories that speaks directly to the redeeming, transforming power of the Lord Jesus Christ.

We see this sentiment repeated even at the end of time when John said: *"And they have conquered by the blood of the Lamb and by the word of their testimony..."* (Revelation 12:11). The beauty of our Author God is that He never wastes a story. He is careful and purposeful with every story so that we might point back, in victory, to our triumphant Savior and Hero. Every redeemed life becomes part of the victory chorus as a living testimony that declares the power of the blood of the Lamb. Our stories don't just tell *what we've survived; they proclaim who He is*. They stand like Joshua's memorial stone to proclaim the goodness and power of God!

What a beautiful thing that God not only writes our stories, but He writes our stories to be a reflection of His story— the story He's been crafting since the dawn of Creation.

The Story Only He Could Write

As The Hero's Journey involves human qualities, Jesus overcame some of the hardest parts of that plotline without the typical human responses we discussed in the previous chapters. There's something profoundly comforting about knowing the One writing our story has lived the *perfect story*. From His humble birth to His victorious resurrection, Jesus' life is the most accurate picture of what it means to trust the Father's hand completely. He never feared. He never sulked away. He never doubted the abilities God gave Him. He knew His calling and His purpose, and He walked straight into it with steadfast determination in each step. He didn't just *tell* us how to walk by faith; He *showed* us, step by step, how to surrender every page of His earthly story to the divine Author's will.

From the very beginning, His life defied all expectations. The Messiah didn't arrive with fanfare or political power as was expected by the religious "experts." Instead, He made His entrance into this world through the quiet obedience of a young woman in a small, unassuming town. Heaven's King entered through humanity's back door. He didn't come dressed in royal robes but in swaddling clothes. That's how God writes His most excellent chapters: with *humility born from the hidden places*.

Jesus holds a beautiful mystery in His existence—both eternally and earthly—in that He embodies the truest Hero embarking on the most epic of quests. If we study what we know from John 1:1 (*"In the beginning was the Word..."* who is Jesus) through Revelation 22 (where Jesus stands victorious at the end of time), we can plot out the mystery of The Hero's Journey. We can also look at Jesus' life in Heaven (before descending to earth) through His life, ministry, death, resurrection, and ascension, and we can again see the plotline of The Hero's Journey. We can zoom in even further and look just at His three years of ministry here on earth, which stands as another testament to God's use of this divine plotline! Jesus really *is* the divine Hero of God's perfect plotline. All other plotlines are written to point to Him, as well.

For the sake of space and time, in this book, we will only look at the smallest portion of Jesus' divine plotline through His earthly ministry. When Jesus began His ministry, He did so in *total* dependence on the Father, His mentor and guide. Every miracle, every message, every moment flowed from the intimacy of prayer and obedience. Even in the forty days of wilderness — when hunger and temptation pressed hard — He refused to write His own way out. He leaned on and trusted the Author's words: *"Man shall not live by bread alone"* (Matthew 4:4). Time and time again throughout His ministry, He released valuable truths on how to walk The Hero's Journey in humble submission to the will of the Father. Jesus understood something we often forget: the Father's story is always better than our shortcuts.

Surrender in the Garden

As His journey unfolded, so did the weight of misunderstanding. Those He came to save often rejected Him, some with hostility and death threats pouring from their mouths like a serpent's venom. The crowds who once shouted "Hosanna!" soon turned to "Crucify Him!" His closest friends fell asleep in His darkest hour, and one of them even betrayed Him for silver! Yet, through it all, Jesus kept walking the path marked out for Him: the path that led straight from Gethsemane to Calvary.

In the Garden of Gethsemane, we see something inspirational, beautiful, and humbling in our Hero. There, beneath the olive trees, we see Jesus release the most vulnerable prayer in Scripture: *"Father, if You are willing, remove this cup from Me. Nevertheless, not My will, but Yours, be done"* (Luke 22:42). Jesus felt the fear. He knew—and dreaded—what was to come upon Him: torture, excruciating pain, abandonment of the Father, and a horrific death. Yet, He didn't reject the call. He acknowledged the fear and agony *("My soul is very sorrowful, even to death..."* Matthew 26:28 and *"...being in agony He prayed more earnestly; and His sweat became like great drops of blood falling down to the ground"* Luke 22:44) and still chose to say, *"Father, if You are willing, let this cup pass from Me; nevertheless, not My will, but Yours be done"* (Luke 22:42). Jesus chose absolute surrender. In the midst of His darkest hour— experiencing the pain of abandonment from the Father, which **none of us will ever have to experience**— Jesus still chose to surrender!

He trusted the Father's masterful story over His own desire for release. Jesus understood better than anyone else the beauty and power of the Father's will and how He incorporates all things together for good. In that moment, the Son submitted His story entirely into the Father's hands. He didn't fight the Author's pen — He trusted it. He chose surrender over self-preservation. And that surrender changed everything for Him *and for us.*

The Cross and the Empty Tomb

At the cross, the story simultaneously reached its lowest valley and its highest victory. This was Jesus' absolute ordeal. The One who spoke worlds into being (Remember, John 1:1 *"In the beginning was the Word. The Word was with God, and the Word was God…"*) allowed Himself to be silenced. The hands that healed the blind, deaf, leper, and lame were pierced. The voice that called Lazarus from the tomb went quiet.

But the Author wasn't silent. The Author was writing.

Three days later, in the most potent and tremendous display of heroic resurrection, the stone rolled away. The story that looked like defeat became the greatest redemption ever told. The empty tomb became proof of His power *and* the promise of our own spiritual resurrection and redemption! It declared and echoed throughout time this triumphant proclamation: **No chapter surrendered to God ever ends in death.**

The Ongoing Story of Grace

Looking at the path of The Hero's Journey, Jesus conquered the ordeal, and He rose again in absolute victory. This speaks to the power He holds even over each of our own journeys. He is victorious. Jesus went through all of the pains we have discussed in this book: the refining fire, the Potter's crushing, the wilderness season, betrayal, waiting, and persecution. None of it overcame Him. He overcame them all! Now, He stands with hands extended to each of us, saying, "I've been there. I know the pain, the struggle, and the heartbreak. But I'm here with you now. You are not alone in this trial! I will walk every step with you. And when you've gone through this? You are going to be a new creation. You are going to be victorious. And the fruit of your trial is going to be robust, glorious, and sweeter than you could've ever imagined. Trust me. I am with you." This is the most beautiful invitation into the unknown, and it comes to us from the Hero who walked with perfection through the most challenging journey of all.

When Jesus rose and later ascended to heaven, He didn't set down the pen and close the book. Instead, He commissioned *us* to keep living His story, to carry His message, and to extend His mercy to the rest of Creation. He invites us to reflect His glory by allowing the Author of Life to now write through us. This very thought makes me weep as I write this! Jesus—who suffered such agony, who conquered death and sin, who stands victorious in Heaven—looks now at His precious ones with anticipation. He doesn't see broken vessels or tarnished stories. He doesn't see hopeless messes whom He cannot redeem or use. He sees promise and potential. He sees a story still being written by the divine Author.

Because He is not only the Author but also the **Finisher**, we can rest assured that every page of our lives—even the ones filled with suffering, silence, pain, or uncertainty—is moving toward His perfect, masterfully-written conclusion. Be encouraged, friend. No matter what you are facing right now. He understands. When we face rejection, He understands. When we wrestle with obedience, He's been there. When we surrender our will, we meet Him in that same Gethsemane grace. Our story is safe in the hands of the One who already wrote the ending.

Not Just Another Biblical Example

Jesus isn't simply another Biblical example of The Hero's Journey. He's the **embodiment and fulfillment** of all the themes that appeared in the other lives we studied. His life both culminates and completes the spiritual truths we have been building throughout this book. Jesus is the fulfillment of every story, the embodiment of every virtue, and the perfect expression of what each man only foreshadowed. Each of the men we've studied in *The Divine Plotline* revealed a glimpse of God's character — a shadow of the greater story that would one day be fulfilled in Jesus. Every act of obedience, every trial endured, and every triumph of faith from these seven men (and countless others in the Bible) was a faint echo of the One who would embody them all *perfectly*. Jesus is the greater Job, the true Abraham, the better Joseph, the perfect Moses, the triumphant Joshua, the rightful David, and the transformed Paul.

Job's suffering tested his faith, but his story ends with restoration. Jesus entered a far deeper darkness than Job experienced (bearing the full weight of sin and separation on the cross), and He trusted the Father's plan perfectly. Like Job, Jesus was "blameless and upright," yet He endured agony to cleanse us from our sins. And when the darkness lifted, His resurrection brought both His own restoration *and* the redemption of all creation. We see a direct foreshadowing of Job's words in Jesus' words: *"Though He slay me, yet will I trust Him"* (Job 13:15) was fulfilled in *"Father, into Your hands I commit My spirit"* (Luke 23:46).

Abraham obeyed when he didn't know where he was going. Jesus obeyed when He knew precisely where it would lead: the cross. Abraham walked toward promise; Jesus walked toward sacrifice. In both, faith triumphed over fear. Abraham believed God for one son; Jesus became the sacrifice through which *many sons* would be brought to glory. Again, we see the foreshadowing in Abraham's story completed in this: *"By faith Abraham obeyed..."* (Hebrews 11:8), and in Christ we see obedience perfected: *"Not My will, but Yours be done"* (Luke 22:42).

Joseph's life was a story of betrayal, false accusation, and divine elevation. Jesus, too, was betrayed by those closest to Him, falsely condemned, and yet exalted to the highest throne. We see the completion of Joseph's story in Jesus! Joseph forgave his brothers, saying, *"What you meant for evil, God meant for good"* (Genesis 50:20). Jesus, hanging on the cross, spoke the greater forgiveness: *"Father, forgive them, for they know not what they do"* (Luke 23:34). Through Joseph, we saw glimpses of redemption; in Jesus, redemption itself was born.

Moses foreshadowed God's deliverance when he led God's people out of bondage; Jesus delivered an even greater, absolute deliverance for humanity from sin itself. Moses met God in the wilderness and spoke with Him face to face; Jesus *was* God, entering *our* wilderness so that we might meet Him personally. Moses gave the law; Jesus fulfilled it. The wilderness that tested Moses became the world Jesus entered—to show us that every barren place can become holy ground when God is present there. In the Book of John, we see that Jesus fulfilled the foreshadowing brought through Moses: *"The law was given through Moses; grace and truth came through Jesus Christ"* (John 1:17).

Joshua led Israel into their promised land; Jesus leads His people into eternal victory, the divine Promised Land. Both of these men stood on the edge of battle with courage that came from God's presence: *"Be strong and courageous... for the Lord your God is with you"* (Joshua 1:9). Jesus embodied that courage as He faced the cross—the greatest battle ever fought—and said, *"...nevertheless, not My will, but Yours be done"* (Luke 22:42). Through Jesus' courageous defiance of fear, He conquered sin and death once for all. Joshua's sword brought temporary peace; Jesus' sacrifice brought everlasting peace. The walls that fell in Jericho were only a shadow of the greater wall Jesus would break: the veil that stood as a wall between God and man.

David's story was one of hidden anointing, years of waiting, and triumphing through worship. Jesus, too, was the anointed King long before the world recognized Him. Jesus, too, faced rejection, persecution, and betrayal, yet continued to worship and obey the Father. David refused to take the throne by force; Jesus declined to seize earthly power, choosing instead a crown of thorns. David's kingdom rose and fell, but Jesus' kingdom will never end. We see the foreshadowing from David's life perfectly fulfilled in Jesus in David's Psalm: *"My God, my God, why have you forsaken me?"* (Psalm 22:1). This is the cry David penned in distress and is also the very words Jesus spoke from the cross (Matthew 27:46). This shows that David's deepest agony foreshadowed Christ's own, yet in both, **trust remained unbroken and victory was won**.

Paul's story is one of radical transformation: a religious zealot turned servant, a persecutor turned preacher. Jesus never needed transformation, but through His grace, He transforms all who meet Him—including Paul! Paul's encounter on the Damascus road mirrors humanity's encounter with Christ: light breaking into darkness, truth shattering pride, and love rewriting the story. Every conversion is a reflection of that same miracle. Jesus' life, death, and resurrection, is perfectly reflected in Paul's transformation: the old passes away, and the new begins (2 Corinthians 5:17). Paul would later summarize the miracle of his transformation in one powerful verse *"I have been crucified with Christ. It is no longer I who live, but Christ who lives in me"* (Galatians 2:20). Paul's old identity died on that Damascus road, and in its place, Christ's life took root. This is the clearest proof that grace doesn't just forgive us; it remakes us.

The Fulfillment of Every Story

Each of these men foreshadowed a part of the divine plotline, and Jesus is the fullness of it. He trusted through suffering like Job, obeyed by faith like Abraham, forgave like Joseph, delivered like Moses, conquered like Joshua, reigned like David, and transformed lives like Paul. Every thread of Scripture weaves back to Him, the Perfect Hero. And every story—including yours—finds its resolution in Him.

Key Themes from the Life of Jesus

1. Perfect Obedience to the Father's Will

From His first public moment at baptism to His final breath on the cross, Jesus lived in *full* submission to the Father. His life demonstrates that true holiness is born from a surrendered relationship with the Father. This sentiment is most keenly seen when Jesus prayed, *"Not My will, but Yours be done"* (Luke 22:42). Through His obedience, we know what it truly means to trust the Author with every page—even the scariest and most painful ones.

2. Humility as the Path to Glory

Jesus' story began in a manger and climaxed on a cross. These two items—the manager and the cross—are both symbols of Jesus' humility. Despite their lowly positions, both became platforms for Heaven's most significant victories through Jesus. Jesus Himself taught this principle when He preached, *"If anyone would be first, he must be last of all and servant of all"* (Mark 9:35). He showed us that the way *up* in God's kingdom is always *down*, through servanthood, sacrifice, and surrender.

3. Suffering That Redeems

Every other hero we have discussed endured suffering. One of my favorite things about Jesus as our Perfect Hero is that, although He also endured suffering, Jesus redeemed suffering. His pain was not accidental but purposeful! His ordeal was the divine exchange where our sin met His righteousness. Because He entered into our brokenness, we can now find beauty and redemption in our own trials. The cross reframes our pain as participation in His story of victory.

4. Love That Chooses the Cross

Love is the thread that runs through every scene of Jesus' life. He touched the untouchable, forgave the unforgivable, and embraced the outcast. But the greatest expression of His love was not found in His miracles. No, His greatest expression of His love was in His willingness to die: *"Greater love has no one than this, that someone lay down his life for his friends"* (John 15:13). At the cross, we see the Author Himself writing love into the pages of our redemption.

5. Resurrection Power That Transforms All Things

The resurrection, although the most important historical event to ever take place, is more than just "history." His resurrection is the very heartbeat of our faith. Jesus didn't *just* rise from death; He forever changed death's power and meaning. Now, death is no longer the end of someone's story when it is surrendered to Him. Every surrendered life becomes a reflection of the assurance that God brings beauty from ashes and life from what seems lost.

6. The Ongoing Story of His Spirit

Just as the death and resurrection weren't the end of Jesus' story, so Jesus' ascension also wasn't the end! This was just the beginning of the next chapter. From there, He sent His Spirit to dwell amongst and within believers, ensuring that *His story continues in and through us*. We are not merely recipients of redemption; we are participants in it! What a beautiful invitation! We are the living chapters of the divine plotline He began. Each act of obedience, every step of faith, every surrendered "yes" adds another paragraph to the story He's still writing. Our personal stories are not just our own. They have added chapters to His story. And THAT is an eye-opening, powerful realization to embrace.

Pause on the Path

Jesus is not only the Author of our stories but also the Perfect Hero who walked the journey before us. In every hard season of surrender, we can look to Him as our example and our strength. Because He conquered sin and death, we can face our own challenges with faith, knowing that the same power that raised Him from the dead is at work within us. Praise the Lord!

When you're feeling at your lowest, remember that you are not alone: *"For we do not have a high priest who is unable to sympathize with our weaknesses, but one who in every respect has been tempted as we are, yet without sin"* (Hebrews 4:15). When we understand Jesus as our Perfect Hero—the One who endured and faced the whole arc of the journey *and* emerged victorious—it changes how we walk through our own story.

Reflecting on His example will transform our perspective. When we approach our own seasons of hardship by looking to His journey for hope and strength, the miraculous happens. Surrender no longer feels like loss. Obedience no longer feels like limitation. Hardship no longer feels wasted. Instead of responding to the stories we find ourselves in with self-pity, anger, "That's Not Fair," self-punishment, apathy, or "Not today, Satan," we can respond with renewed hope, strength, faith, and determination to fulfill the journey.

In seeing Jesus' life as the completed Hero's Journey, we realize that every fiery trial and broken moment is an opportunity to respond like Him: with holiness, trust, submission, and humility. Our goal isn't to escape the hard chapters but to echo His heart within them and to glorify Him through them.

Putting It into Practice

Write: Take time to journal about your current "Gethsemane" — a place where you feel stretched, pressed, or uncertain. What would it look like to echo Jesus' words in that place: *"Nevertheless, not my will, but Yours be done"* (Luke 22:42)? Write down your honest fears and then surrender them to God on paper.

Pray: Pray that the Lord would give you a heart that mirrors Jesus' obedience. Ask Him to help you see your hardships as a holy training ground where He is shaping you. Invite the Holy Spirit to strengthen your resolve to trust the Author's pen even when you can't see the next line.

Act: This week, practice obedience in one specific area you've been resisting. It might be forgiving someone, releasing control, or stepping into something that requires courage. Choose to respond to your current trial with the heart posture of Christ — humble, faithful, and wholly surrendered.

Declare: Speak this truth over your life: *"For from Him and through Him and to Him are all things. To Him be glory forever. Amen"* (Romans 11:36). Then, add this declaration of personal faith: "My life is being written by the Author who already finished the story. I will trust Him with this page." To take this a step further, write down Romans 11:36

along with this personal declaration on a notecard. Put it somewhere you will see it every day.

Prayer for the Journey

Jesus, my Perfect Hero, You walked the path before me. You trusted, obeyed, and surrendered fully to the Father's will. Teach me to respond to my own trials with the same grace and courage that You displayed. Help me to see my hardships as invitations towards deeper intimacy with You. When I am tempted to take control of my story, remind me that You have already written redemption into every line. May my life reflect Your character. May my suffering mirror Your surrender! May my story point back to Your glory. I surrender my life to your masterful pen, Lord. In Jesus' name, Amen.

CHAPTER 18

Growing In Our Responses To The Potter's Hands

Now that we have received some fresh perspective on the Journey of Jesus, I encourage you to surrender your story to Him as we move into the last few chapters of this book. He surrendered everything for us, and now, in response to His ultimate sacrifice, we, too, must submit everything to Him—even the hardest challenges. In my own life, I have lived the lowest, ugliest responses to Jesus, and, in recent trials, have experienced heartbreaking triumph and a growing relationship with Jesus. It's only through Jesus that we can truly overcome our hardest, darkest seasons with hope and joy—despite the circumstances or outcomes.

In October of 2024, my husband and I were receiving prophetic ministry at a Presbytery that our church was hosting. Three trusted men of God came to our church and prophesied over different couples and individuals. During that presbytery, one of the men said that our family would be growing into a "full" family. Before this, we had decided that our family was complete. But God must have had other plans! In December of 2024, I learned that we were unexpectedly pregnant. It was unplanned, surprising, and very exciting.

In January of 2025 (the year I began writing this book), I had my first doctor's appointment. At this appointment, we did not get the news we wanted. We were told that our baby had already died—probably around week seven or eight. Our excitement quickly turned to heartbreak. However, I was not convinced this was the end of our baby's story. I began to pray fervently for a miraculous answer from the Lord.

A week later, we had another appointment. We received only heartwrenching confirmation that the baby had indeed died. I was still not ready to give up hope. My body still hadn't shown any signs of miscarriage, and I was still feeling all the first-trimester symptoms in all their unpleasant glory. In the midst of this, I stood firm in my faith. In past trials, I would have responded with horrible negativity. This time, I found myself turning to the Lord, instead of twisting within myself in negative emotions. Don't get me wrong: I felt the feelings! I felt them deeply. My heart was absolutely breaking as I interceded and begged for the life of my child. I even offered my own life up in exchange if God would just give my baby the chance to live.

Finally, later that month, my body began the process of dispelling the miscarriage. I had received my answer from the Lord. It was *not* the answer I so desperately desired. I was heartbroken and grieving; however, my heart remained tender towards the Lord.

After a few days of passing the miscarriage, all hell broke loose within my body. One Sunday morning, while the rest of my family went to church, my one-year-old son and I stayed home because I wasn't feeling great due to the miscarriage. While I was in the shower, my body began massively hemorrhaging blood. Within minutes, I was slumped on the floor of my shower with my one-year-old son right beside me in the kiddy bathtub. I knew I was in a perilous predicament. I looked across the bathroom to my phone on the counter. With all of my remaining strength and through blurred, swirling vision, I crawled across the bathroom floor to retrieve my phone. I called my husband, a nurse, who thankfully was just minutes away from home. He rushed upstairs to help me and immediately saw how dire the situation was. He tried to help me stand up, so I could get to the hospital. My body finally gave out, and I collapsed heavily upon the floor. I felt life leaving my body. I couldn't move. I could barely breathe. My world was spinning into darkness. All I could muster to say was "Jesus, help me." I prayed that simple prayer with every weakening breath I had.

When the EMTs arrived, my vital signs were critically low and quickly declining. They rushed me to the hospital where they were able to stabilize my vitals. On top of the horrifying feeling of death crouching at my life's doorstep, I was also experiencing horrible labor contractions as my body was desperately trying to eliminate the remaining "conception debris," as the hospital called it. After two attempts to stop the bleeding from two different doctors in the emergency room (while being awake! That was awful), the surgeon called for an emergency surgery. I was taken to surgery and put under anesthesia. When I awakened, the bleeding had stopped, the chaos had subsided, and my body had stabilized. I felt such relief as I laid in the recovery room thanking Jesus for saving me.

After a couple of hours of observation, the hospital gave me an option: stay the night for a blood transfusion and further observation, or go home and begin my long, slow recovery. I couldn't wait to get *out* of there! After a horrible, long day of facing death—both of my unborn child and myself—I was finally able to go home. I felt incredibly weak and groggy. Standing was a chore; walking was a downright struggle. And on top of all the physical pain and discomfort, my heart was broken from the finality of the loss of my child. My husband and I spent the next several weeks grieving the loss of our baby as my body slowly recovered.

In the midst of all of this, God altogether showed up and transformed my heart. Not once did I feel anger or resentment towards God. I cherished the breath He gave me, and time became a much more valuable commodity in my heart. Superficial aspirations or uses of my time fell by the wayside as God used this terrifying experience to rearrange my life's priorities. I look back now at those early months of 2025 to see how much God has done in my heart over the previous eight years. Where I used to respond to the hardships of life with any of the typical responses we discussed in the previous chapters, I found myself leaning into the presence of God with a more profound desire to submit my life and circumstances to His hand. I encountered the beautiful comfort from the Lord in my darkest hour of grief and loss. In the months following my ordeal, God met me in recovery and weakness and revealed the essence of this book to me. From that trial, He breathed something entirely fresh into my life.

Additionally, the Lord revealed to me that the child we lost was a son. We gave him the name "David," which means "beloved." Sometimes

I imagine our sweet David running and playing in the fields of Heaven with the angels and with other children who were taken too soon. I imagine his smile, his eyes, and his laugh. It gives me joy to know that the Father of Creation is my baby's Father in Heaven. And I feel such peace. The pain is still there. Even long after, I still shed tears when I think about my baby son, whom I won't get to meet until I myself get to Heaven. However, I trust God's plan and purpose for my life.

Since the loss of our baby, David, God has blessed us with another baby boy: Josiah, who made his entrance into this world in November, 2025. What's even more special? One of the very men who prophesied over us in fall of 2024 came back to our church while I was pregnant with Josiah, and—in an exciting turn of events—called me out of the congregation and prophesied over my unborn Josiah. He spoke of God's call on His life as a worshipper in the House of the Lord.

Although my circumstances may not be as painful as others have been through (I think of Job's story and other stories, as well), I can certainly attest to the molding and transforming power of God in my life through the pain of abuse, divorce, and my own Hero's Journey. God didn't remove the pain of the loss of my son, David, but He also restored unto me another son, Josiah. God already has His hand on this child's life, as He has spoken words of encouragement and prophetic vision over him.

How Does God Want Me to Respond to His Pruning?

Precious reader, I want to encourage you: God's transformative journey takes time. The length of that journey will vary from person to person, too! It's important to never compare your story to that of others. It's so easy to fall into comparison: "So-and-So went through something similar, and it only lasted months. Why am I still trudging along on this journey?!" Don't let yourself get caught in that trap! When you might be tempted to think and feel this way, please look back at the lives of the men in the Bible who endured The Hero's Journey to various lengths. Abraham's journey was twenty-five years. Moses experienced *two* journeys, each lasting forty years! Joseph waited twenty-two years. David waited fifteen years. And many others in the Bible waited and waited for the Lord to bring resolution and answers to their journeys. Our journeys will each vary in length. So, as tempting as it may be, when you're in the wilderness and in the waiting, don't compare your story to someone else's story. Your story is your own, and God has crafted it just for you. He knows what you need to be molded into the person He desires you to be.

We are each on a beautiful, unique journey that the Potter takes us through to break us down and reshape us from vessels of dishonor to vessels of honor (Romans 9:21). Here's another important truth I want you to put in your heart: no one simply "arrives" with perfect wisdom and understanding of the journey after only one season of hardship. Our Potter knows to be gentle with us and mold us softly and carefully - never giving us more than we can handle (yes, even the gut-wrenching seasons of life). He is with us through even the darkest valley, just like David wrote in his most-famous Psalm: *"Even though I walk through the valley of the shadow of death, I will fear no evil, for you are with me; your rod and your staff, they comfort me"* (Psalm 23:4). It's not a matter of *if* you will encounter The Hero's Journey, but *when*. Trials are not interruptions to the Christian life. They are part of God's transformative plan.

Regardless of your particular journey, God wants us to respond to His journey in a Biblical manner. Our first responses will often echo the flawed patterns we discussed earlier: self-pity, anger, apathy, or blaming Satan, but Scripture calls us higher. God invites us to grow *in* the journey as much as *through* it. Rather than fighting, avoiding, or sulking through hardship, the Bible points us to better responses—ones that reflect trust, endurance, and surrender to His hand. Here are a few of the ways God calls His children and servants to respond:

1. Respond with Trust and Surrender

For God's most whole work to be accomplished in us, we must lay down our old ways of thinking and respond with trust and surrender. God's full and complete refining work requires faith that *His hands are good, even when His methods feel hard.* Trials are not a sign of His absence but proof of His active fatherly care. The same is true of natural, earthly parenting. If I love my children (which I can assure you, I DO!), I won't let them act in specific ways or let them do certain things that are dangerous to them, physically or emotionally. If my toddler, who is full of spunk and fire, screams "No!!!" in my face when I tell him to stop doing something dangerous, I discipline him. As much as he may cry and throw a fit about discipline, as his mom, I know that discipline is far more important than appeasing his anger. The fruit of obedience I desire to grow in my son is of utmost importance over the temporary appeasement of his fiery, toddler emotions.

God knows the same thing for us. Even when the pain seems unbearable, and we might want to scream and yell at God, we must start responding to His hand with **trust and surrender!** This is taught to us so clearly in Proverbs, when God reminds us to *"Trust in the Lord with all your heart and lean not on your own understanding; in all your ways submit to him, and he will make your paths straight"* (Proverbs 3:5-6). He reiterates this truth through Paul's writings to the Roman church: *"We know that for those who love God **all things work together for good**, for those who are called according to his purpose"* (Romans 8:28). God uses "all things" to transform us into the image of His Son – yes, even the ugliest, hardest seasons of our lives. Our job now is to take this Biblical truth and attach it as a tool to the Belt of Truth (Ephesians 6:11-17). Never let that truth leave you! Rest in that truth, so that when the storms come, we can respond with trust and surrender.

2. Persevere with Joyful Endurance

Notice that this isn't just saying "with endurance." This isn't an apathetic response of "Oh, I'm just enduring until this passes me by!" We already addressed that flawed response in the last chapter. Instead, *joyful endurance* is entirely different. It's holding onto hope with the joy of knowing God is at work in us. *THIS* is truly how we can *"Consider it pure joy… because you know that the testing of your faith produces perseverance. Let perseverance finish its work so that you may be mature and complete…"* (James 1:2-4). When we realize God's pruning means transformation into His glory, endurance becomes an exciting invitation.

Does that mean that there won't be pain and hardship? Not at all. But it does mean we can walk through the pain and hardship with our heads lifted in trust and surrender to the Heavenly King whose ways are higher than ours. We can approach the pain knowing there will be beautiful fruit on the other side of the journey! It really is an exciting thing to know that the God of creation has focused on growing and maturing *you* for His kingdom. We see this in the life of Jesus! Jesus, who experienced tremendous pain and persecution to the point of a horrible death on the cross, considered His journey a joy. This is expressed in Hebrews, which says, *"Looking to Jesus, the founder and perfecter of our faith, **who for the joy that was set before him endured the cross**, despising the shame, and is seated at the right hand of the throne of God* (Hebrews 12:2). Yes, Jesus considered it a joy to walk through the persecution of the cross, because He *knew the outcome:* He would be seated at the right hand of God – victorious over death and sin!

3. Humble Yourself and Receive His Discipline

Hardship can be God's loving discipline. When He disciplines and prunes areas of weakness or sin out of our lives, that's a sign that we truly belong to Him. The author of Hebrews teaches us this truth:

> "... *The Lord disciplines the one he loves, and chastises every son whom he receives. It is for discipline that you have to endure. God is treating you as sons. For what son is there whom his father does not discipline?* **If you are left without discipline, in which all have participated, then you are illegitimate children** *and not sons.... For the moment, all discipline seems painful rather than pleasant, but* **later it yields the peaceful fruit of righteousness** *to those who have been trained by it"* (Hebrews 12:5-7, 11).

Discipline is for our good, so that we may share in His holiness!

Have you ever encountered a child who, upon receiving correction and discipline, reacts with defiance and pride? I may or may not have been one of *those* particular types of kids myself. Oh, the joys of parenting! In the moment, whether you are the parent administering the discipline or the child receiving it, it may feel unpleasant. The reality is that healthy discipline is a sign of love. Of course, I am not referring to angry outbursts or abusive behavior. Healthy **discipline is done from a heart of love** that says, "I see great potential in you, and your behavior is poisoning your future. Let me correct this in you and for you." God does the same thing for us. Psalm 119 says, *"It was good for me to be afflicted so that I might learn your decrees"* (Psalm 119:71). God knows the areas of our hearts that need correction and pruning. Our job is to humble our hearts to receive His correction and discipline—even when it hurts tremendously. When we respond in pride and defiance (much like the typical responses we discussed in the last chapter), we prolong our pruning and waste our suffering.

4. Keep Serving and Bearing Fruit

Maturity in Christ means we don't stop serving Him until the hardship "passes." This is the mindset of apathy! As you and I are growing out of the typical responses birthed from our flesh, we need to remain faithful in small things *right where we are*. God isn't asking us for a mindblowing, dramatic transformation in the blink of an eye. He is much more gracious than that. He simply desires for us to "*not become weary in doing good, for at the proper time we will reap a harvest if we do not give up*" (Galatians 6:9). God wants us to keep our eyes on Him and keep serving Him! He wants our hearts, our trust, our service, our attention, and our time. He wants us to stand firm *in Him*. He wants you to always give yourself fully to the work of the Lord. Trust. Serve. And watch the fruit of your life blossom, grow, and turn into a bountiful harvest.

5. Let the Trial Drive You Deeper into Christ

As you keep your eyes fixed on Him and respond to the Potter's hands in worship, trust, and submission, the seasons of hardship quickly become invitations to know Christ more intimately through dependence on Him. Gone are the days of anger, apathy, or self-pity. Instead, when a new trial comes into your life, you will find yourself embracing the pruning with the strength and joy of the Lord. With proper focus—your eyes on Jesus—the trials begin to become opportunities for intimacy with Jesus. Not to say they won't still be hard. Still, when the difficulties strike, like David, you must "*strengthen [yourself] in the Lord [your] God*" (1 Samuel 30:6). This is such a powerful example of turning directly to God for courage and renewed hope when everything feels like it's collapsing.

It's easy to ask "*Why?*" when calamities strike your life. However, in the midst of your *Why?*, remember to focus on the *Who?* of who God is and His purposes! You don't really need to know why—outside of "This is another opportunity for God to tenderize my heart towards Him, to grow deeper intimacy with the King, and to grow in Christ-like maturity." When you begin to see the trials of life as opportunities to be driven into deeper, intimate relationship with the Lord, you begin to unlock the truth behind the numerous Bible verses that discuss having *joy* in the midst of trials:

- **James 1:2–4** "*Consider it pure joy, my brothers and sisters, whenever you face trials of many kinds, because you know that the testing of your faith produces perseverance. Let perseverance finish its work so that you may be mature and complete, not lacking anything.*"

- **John 15:2** "*He cuts off every branch in me that bears no fruit, while every branch that does bear fruit he prunes so that it will be even more fruitful.*"

- **1 Peter 1:6–7** *"In all this you greatly rejoice, though now for a little while you may have had to suffer grief in all kinds of trials. These have come so that the proven genuineness of your faith—of greater worth than gold, which perishes even though refined by fire—may result in praise, glory, and honor when Jesus Christ is revealed."*

- **Philippians 3:8–10** *"Indeed, I count everything as loss because of the surpassing worth of knowing Christ Jesus my Lord. For his sake I have suffered the loss of all things and count them as rubbish, so that I may gain Christ... that I may know him and the power of his resurrection, and may share his sufferings, becoming like him in his death."*

How Do I Recognize the Hand of the Potter in My Life?

A crucial question that needs to be addressed before moving on is this: "How do I know if the trial I am facing is from God's molding hand, an attack of the enemy, or just a part of this world we live in?" Let's address some key steps you need to begin implementing in your life as the trials and difficulties of life come your way.

1. Examine the Fruit It's Producing

- If the difficulty is pressing you toward **repentance, humility, holiness, and deeper dependence on God**, it is often the Lord's loving discipline or maturing work.

- If it's driving you toward **doubt, despair, anger, temptation, or rebellion**, it may be a spiritual attack — though God can still redeem even that for your growth (isn't God so good?).

- If it's simply a **frustrating reality** of life in a broken world (illness, decay, death), it may not have a moral cause, but God can still use it to form Christ in you.

    - For example, just because you hit another red light and have been stuck in traffic for hours doesn't make it an attack of the enemy or God trying to transform you. However, God can still use that situation to grow your patience and trust!

Here are some key verses to help you determine the fruit of your trial:

- **Matthew 7:17–18** – *"So, every healthy tree bears good fruit, but the diseased tree bears bad fruit. A healthy tree cannot bear bad fruit, nor can a diseased tree bear good fruit."*

- **Galatians 5:22–23** – *"But the fruit of the Spirit is love, joy, peace, patience, kindness, goodness, faithfulness, gentleness, self-control; against such things there is no law."*

- **Ephesians 5:9–10** – *"(for the fruit of light is found in all that is good and right and true), and try to discern what is pleasing to the Lord."*

- **James 3:17** – *"But the wisdom from above is first pure, then peaceable, gentle, open to reason, full of mercy and good fruits, impartial and sincere."*

- **John 15:8** – *"By this my Father is glorified, that you bear much fruit and so prove to be my disciples."*

2. Test It Against God's Word

God's discipline and refining will always align with His Word and character. The enemy's attacks often distort Scripture or tempt us toward sin. When the trials come your way, *run to God's Word!*

- If you sense the hardship is **calling you to obey, surrender, or trust** more fully in Christ, it's consistent with God's work.

- If the pressure **leads you to disobedience, bitterness, or a compromise** of God's truth, it's not from Him. However, you can still correct your heart's response and allow the Lord to use that attack to grow and mature you!

Here are some key verses to help you look at how your trial might line up with God's Word:

- **1 John 4:1** – *"Do not believe every spirit, but test the spirits to see whether they are from God."*

- **2 Timothy 3:16–17** – *"All Scripture is breathed out by God and profitable for teaching, for reproof, for correction, and for training in righteousness, that the man of God may be complete, equipped for every good work."*

- **Psalm 119:105** – *"Your word is a lamp to my feet and a light to my path."*

- **Acts 17:11** – *"...they received the word with all eagerness, examining the Scriptures daily to see if these things were so."*

- **John 17:17** – *"Sanctify them in the truth; your word is truth."*

3. Look at the Source and Nature of Opposition

There is always going to be a subtle voice beneath every trial. The voice you hear can have three primary sources: God's voice, Satan's voice, or the voice of your flesh. Listen closely to what that voice is whispering to you. Don't be so quick to obey that voice; just listen. Examine the words. Then, assess the origin of the voice.

- The enemy's attacks often target your faith, your identity in Christ, and your mission for God's kingdom (Ephesians 6:11–12). When trials strike, if you find yourself thinking, "Why am I even doing this? I'm worthless. God could do so much better than me." Or "I'm such an imposter. Some Christian I am!" These thoughts are poison for your soul and can only come from one source.

- God's refining voice will also involve hardship, but His purpose is to remove impurities, not destroy you. His voice will speak with conviction that leads to repentance and a deeper relationship—not isolation! For example, God will never say, "You are bad" (that's the enemy attacking your identity). Rather, God's refining voice will say, "That was bad. Let's talk about this. Bring this to me. And let me fix this within you, so you can better glorify My name." See the difference?

- Some trials, like disease, disasters, or human conflict, can simply be a part of living in a fallen creation (Romans 8:20–22). Even if those trials come, you can still submit them to God for Him to use to refine and mature you, too.

Here are some key verses to help you identify the voice that whispers in the trial:

- **John 10:10** – *"The thief comes only to steal and kill and destroy. I came that they may have life and have it abundantly."*

- **1 Peter 4:12–13** – *"Beloved, do not be surprised at the fiery trial when it comes upon you to test you, as though something strange were happening to you. But rejoice insofar as you share Christ's sufferings, that you may also rejoice and be glad when his glory is revealed."*

- **Romans 8:28** – *"And we know that for those who love God all things work together for good, for those who are called according to his purpose."*

- **James 1:13** – *"Let no one say when he is tempted, 'I am being tempted by God,' for God cannot be tempted with evil, and he himself tempts no one."*

- **1 Peter 5:8** – *"Your adversary the devil prowls around like a roaring lion, seeking someone to devour."*

- **Job 23:10** – *"He knows the way that I take; when he has tried me, I shall come out as gold."*

4. Seek the Holy Spirit's Insight Through Prayer

Ask God directly for clarity on what He's doing! The Spirit gives wisdom to discern whether you're under discipline, attack, or simply living in a broken world – and how to respond in faith *no matter the source*. Remember! Even if the source of the trial is from the devil, the world, or your own flesh, God can still use it to grow you!

- Remember: Sometimes the *why* is hidden, but the *how* (trust and obedience) is *always clear*.

Here are some key verses to help lead you in prayer, seeking the guidance and wisdom of the Holy Spirit:

- **Romans 8:16** – *"The Spirit himself bears witness with our spirit that we are children of God."*

- **James 1:5** – *"If any of you lacks wisdom, let him ask God, who gives generously to all without reproach, and it will be given him."*

- **John 14:26** – *"But the Helper, the Holy Spirit, whom the Father will send in my name, he will teach you all things and bring to your remembrance all that I have said to you."*

- **Romans 8:14** – *"For all who are led by the Spirit of God are sons of God."*

- **1 Corinthians 2:12** – *"Now we have received not the spirit of the world, but the Spirit who is from God, that we might understand the things freely given us by God."*

- **Proverbs 3:5–6** – *"Trust in the Lord with all your heart, and do not lean on your own understanding. In all your ways acknowledge him, and he will make straight your paths."*

5. Submit Your Response, Not Just the Situation

This one is a BIGGY! No matter the source of the trial—whether it be God's molding, Satan's attack, or the world's corruption—God's command is the same: **respond in faith, perseverance, and worship.** Even if you can't say with confidence that you know where the source of the trial is coming from! And if you do believe God is revealing to you the source of the trial, respond appropriately:

- **Discipline?** Repent and realign with His ways. Submit to His hand and His guidance.

- **Attack?** Resist the devil! Get dressed for battle (Ephesians 6:10-20)! Stand firm in truth.

- **Fallen world?** Trust God's promises and endure with hope. Submit the hardship to God to use to transform and mature you from one degree of glory to the next.

Here are some key verses to help you respond to the various sources of the trials:

- **1 Peter 5:6–9** – *"Humble yourselves, therefore, under the mighty hand of God so that at the proper time he may exalt you, casting all your anxieties on him, because he cares for you. Be sober-minded; be watchful. Your adversary, the devil, prowls around like a roaring lion, seeking someone to devour. Resist him, firm in your faith…"*

- **Hebrews 12:11** – *"For the moment all discipline seems painful rather than pleasant, but later it yields the peaceful fruit of righteousness to those who have been trained by it."*

- **Ephesians 6:13** – *"Therefore take up the whole armor of God, that you may be able to withstand in the evil day, and having done all, to stand firm."*

- **Psalm 37:5–6** – *"Commit your way to the Lord; trust in him, and he will act. He will bring forth your righteousness as the light, and your justice as the noonday."*

- **Romans 12:12** – *"Rejoice in hope, be patient in tribulation, be constant in prayer."*

- **James 4:7** - *"Submit yourselves therefore to God. Resist the devil, and he will flee from you."*

Pause on the Path

When trials hit, our first question is often *"Why* is this happening?" Scripture points us to a deeper and more transformative question: *"Lord, what are You transforming in me through this?"* The difference is profound. Asking *why* often traps us in frustration, self-pity, or blame. Asking *"Lord, what are you working on in me?"* shifts our posture to humility and surrender. Scripture invites us to see every hardship as an opportunity to seek God's purposes. It reframes hardship as a tool in the Potter's hands—not as meaningless chaos.

The Bible is full of reminders that trials are not wasted. James tells us to *"consider it pure joy"* when trials come, because God uses them to mature us (James 1:2–4). Paul declares that *"suffering produces perseverance; perseverance, character; and character, hope"* (Romans 5:3–4). Peter reminds us that trials refine our faith like fire refines gold (1 Peter 1:6–7). With each hardship, sometimes it's His refining hand shaping us into Christlikeness, sometimes it's spiritual warfare, and other times it's simply the brokenness of a fallen world.

This perspective calls for a radical shift. Instead of asking God to simply remove the pain, we ask Him to reveal His presence *in* the pain. Instead of demanding answers, we lean into intimacy. Instead of resisting the process, we allow His hands to press, shape, and even break us so that something more beautiful can emerge. Like clay in the hands of the Potter, our role is not to dictate the process, but to yield and trust the One who knows what kind of vessel He is forming us to be (Jeremiah 18:4–6).

So when the storm hits, let your prayer be: *"Lord, I don't understand this, but I trust You. Don't let me waste this pain. Shape me. Refine me. Draw me closer to You."* This is the posture that transforms hardship from a stumbling block into a stepping stone toward Christlikeness. Then, no matter the source of the hardship, the Potter's invitation is always the same: trust Him, stay close, and let Him work in you. And *that*, my friend, is where God does His *best work*.

Putting It Into Practice

Write: Take time to journal about your current or most recent trial. Spend some time praying about where the source of that trial might be coming from. Write out which category you believe it falls into and why, using Scripture to guide your discernment.

Pray: Ask the Lord to give you wisdom (James 1:5) and a heart that is quick to trust Him in any trial.

Act: Begin each day this week with a prayer of surrender: "Lord, shape me and mold me — however You see fit today. I trust you and submit this day to You." Write it down on a piece of paper where you will see it often, or set a reminder on your phone for the same time every day.

When you face difficulty, *pause.* Invite the Holy Spirit to help you discern its source before reacting. Silence your initial emotions and wait for discernment from the Holy Spirit. Don't let your emotions rule your responses.

Set aside a time of personal worship this week — sing, read Psalms, or praise Him aloud — to anchor your heart in His sovereignty.

Share one trial you're going through with a mature believer, asking them to help you see it through a Biblical lens.

Look for at least one way to serve someone else this week — even in your trial — as an act of faith and trust in God's goodness.

Prayer for the Journey

Lord Jesus, thank You for the gift of Your hand upon my life — whether it comes to refine me, protect me, or simply hold me steady in a broken world. Align my heart and my will with Yours, Lord! Teach me to see every trial as an opportunity to know You more deeply. Strengthen me to embrace the trials of this life, not dread or run away or hide from them. Give me wisdom to discern the source, courage to respond in faith, and a heart that worships You no matter the season. Shape me into Your likeness, and let my life be a testimony to Your glory. In Jesus' name, Amen.

CHAPTER 19

Closing Thoughts

This has been quite the journey we have gone through together in this book. I know some of this was hard to read—believe me, it was hard to write! As I wrote, I felt God's strong hand pulling the words out of me, as I relived so much of the pain and hardship that God has brought me through. And, to be honest, I'm still walking through my own journey. None of us ever finishes the race until we pass from this side of Heaven to the other. Although I have grown and matured significantly over the last several years, I still sometimes slip back into old ways of responding to the Lord's pruning.

So, where are *you* at in The Hero's Journey of your own life? Can you look back at difficult seasons for yourself and see the refining steps of God's journey in the midst of your tears and fears? And now, where does the Lord have you right now on *this* journey? There are so many things to discuss and share. I wish we could sit down for coffee so you could pour out your heart to me, just as I have poured my heart out to you through the pages of this book.

Now that you've walked through these chapters and gained a fresh perspective, it's time to move forward in your own journey. Before I close, I want to leave you with a few final thoughts—things that may echo questions already stirring in your heart, or encouragement that I simply can't end this book without sharing. Let's take a look:

Have you missed or ignored any crucial parts of your journey that could be leaving you crippled or slowing you down in your journey?

It is easy to over-analyze your own Hero's Journey! I've done it myself! "Did I miss the mentor? Did I refuse the call, and has God abandoned me? Am I still in the Tests, or is this the Ordeal? What exactly *was* the Reward for that time of my life?" When you feel tempted to over-analyze your story, remember this: no matter where you are, God is still present and working! By providing you with the roadmap of The Hero's Journey, I hope to inspire you to believe that there will always be reward, resurrection, and transformation from your pain. That's just the way God works! I don't want you to get so caught up in figuring out where you're at on the journey that you focus more on the journey *than on the God who walks with you.*

Here's what you can look at in your own journey. For example, did you bypass "Meeting the Mentor," and are you trying to walk this journey without the guidance of the Holy Spirit and the help of the human mentor(s) God has placed in your life? Are you stuck in "Refusal of the Call" and resisting God's attempts to grow you into a new creation? Are you blaming God? Are you praying *against* this seeming-attack of the enemy, instead of embracing God's correcting hand and pruning tools? Are you stuck at "Crossing the First Threshold"? Have you said with your mouth, "Lord, Your will be done," but still refuse in your heart to submit to His will and purpose, thinking you know best? This position of the heart will stop you in your tracks from truly entering into the journey God has planned for you to mold you into the new vessel He desires you to be.

The Lord, rich in grace and mercy, always allows us to return to parts of our journey we may have rushed through, resisted, or tried to do on our own. In fact, if we totally botched a part of our journey, He is pleased to take you back to any point and rework it with you!

God is in the business of story-writing, and *He's not just writing your story.*

God is writing a story in the life of *every single person* on this planet, with the singular goal of bringing each person into a deeper relationship with Him. We so easily get tunnel vision regarding our *own* story that we forget that God is writing a story for everyone else, too.

You are the "hero," or main character, of your own story, but you also play a role in the stories of others' lives, too. Sometimes that may be as a friend, an ally, or a mentor. Sometimes that might even be as an enemy.

For example, when Josh and I were planning our wedding, many of my family members had differing opinions about it. From *my perspective*, my family was in the wrong—*so wrong*—and out of line. From *my* perspective, *they were the enemy of my story*. However, from *their perspective*, I was in the wrong and was the enemy of *their* stories. In the end, God tremendously used that conflict—both sides seeing the other as the enemy in the wrong—to bring *all* parties involved closer to Him! I now look at all the people involved and the relationships we all share, and I see much healthier relationships with one another and a much deeper dependence on God. God allowed that major conflict to come into our family to shake things up, but for each of our own good and for His glory.

When conflict or hardship arises, we must guard against tunnel vision in *our story*. God is writing a far bigger story than just the one you see from your angle. He is carefully crafting *everyone's* stories! He may be using you in someone else's refining process, even as He shapes you in theirs—whether that be as a friend or foe. Don't be so quick to assume that, in every battle, you're the victim! There is a far greater, larger story at work than just your life.

Are you living in a "sequel" to your own journey?

Like the characters in iconic stories with numerous sequels, we don't go through just *one* journey. If you look at stories, like Star Wars or The Hunger Games, the characters in the story go through smaller versions of The Hero's Journey within each book/movie. Then, each smaller story intertwines into its larger, overarching Hero's Journey! The same applies to us. God doesn't do "one and done" stories.

Joseph's life is a powerful Biblical example. His journey didn't end once he was sold into slavery. He went through *multiple cycles* of trials and growth—betrayed by his brothers, falsely accused by Potiphar's wife, forgotten in prison—each one shaping him for the greater calling of saving nations during famine. Each season could be considered a "sequel" to his story, building upon the last until God's purposes were fulfilled.

God, in his sovereignty, wisely breaks our sanctification into seasons. He knows which trials will bear the greatest fruit in us and in His perfect timing. In His grace, He does not call us to walk through all of His transformation in one fell swoop of trials and hardships—that would crush us! He breaks the larger journey of growth into smaller "sequels" to slowly and graciously mature us into His image. He leads us through sequels of growth: one refining fire, one valley, one mountain at a time. Each new cycle builds on the last, stretching our faith a little further, shaping our character a little deeper, and teaching us to rely on Him more fully.

Just because you walk through *one* Hero's Journey cycle doesn't mean you can check the journey off your life's "To Do" list. No, the Potter continues to place us back on His wheel, remolding and reshaping us until the vessel reflects His Son. Sanctification is an ongoing saga in our lives—not a single chapter. God will take you through another cycle when He sees that the time is right. And then another and another! All the while growing and maturing you.

The reality is that every "sequel" carries with it both pain *and* promise. Each one has its own set of trials, but also its own unique rewards: new wisdom, new intimacy with Christ, and new opportunities to bear fruit for His Kingdom. And the final "sequel"? That will only be completed when we step into eternity and hear Him say, *"Well done, good and faithful servant."* Until then, the journey continues because sanctification is a *lifelong* process.

Understanding this whole concept gives radical new meaning and understanding to Paul's letter to the Philippians when he said, "*... for I have learned in whatever situation I am to be content. I know how to be brought low, and I know how to abound. In any and every circumstance, I have learned the secret of facing plenty and hunger, abundance and need.* ***I can do all things through him who strengthens me***" (Philippians 4:11b-

13). This same sentiment is echoed in our key verse in James: *"Consider it pure joy, my brothers and sisters, whenever you face trials of many kinds, because you know that the testing of your faith produces perseverance. Let perseverance finish its work so that you may be mature and complete, not lacking anything"* (James 1:2-4). Trials, hardships, calamities, sickness, struggles, persecution, crushing, and tears *will come*. But, there is hope found in God's divine plotline of The Hero's Journey. That hope is transformation and growth through Him. God *never* abandons us in the journey. The ESSENTIAL key to facing these challenges with joy and confidence is to **lean on our Lord, Jesus Christ,** as the bride leans on her groom in the Song of Solomon: *"Who is that coming up from the wilderness, leaning on her beloved?* (Song of Solomon 8:5a). With Him, we can face ANYTHING that comes our way. That doesn't mean it will be easy or pleasant. It means He will be with us through it all, and *that* is hope worth rejoicing over.

Friend, we've walked through challenging seasons and truths together in these pages – some stormy and jagged, some encouraging and full of light. You've seen that God's storylines are rarely painless or straightforward, but they are *always* purposeful. The truth is, none of us finishes this journey until we step from this life into eternity with Him. That means the refining, pruning, stretching, and growing will continue as long as we have breath.

So let me leave you with this: take a deep breath and remember that your story is still being written. God hasn't set down His pen. He hasn't abandoned you. The trials you face today are not the end; they're the middle chapters that prepare you for the reward, the resurrection, and the transformation that is coming.

The Potter's hands are steady, and His heart toward you is *good*. Whether you are on your first journey, in the middle of a "sequel," or somewhere between battles and blessings, the same God who shaped Job, Abraham, Joseph, Moses, Joshua, David, and Paul is shaping *you*. And you are just as loved and cherished in His eyes as those amazing men of the Bible.

When it feels too heavy to carry on, lean in *close* to Jesus, the One who walks with you through every trial and triumph. He is your Beloved, your strength, and your hope. With Him, you honestly can face anything, like Paul says in Philippians 4:13: *"I can do all things through Christ who strengthens me."* That's not just a trendy sentiment that looks nice on a bumper sticker; it's a promise *anchored* in Scripture, *tested* in the furnace of suffering, and *proven* in the joy of transformation.

So walk forward in your story, not with fear, but with the quiet confidence that your Author is faithful, your story is sacred, and your ending will be glorious.

Pause on the Path

Your life is not a one-and-done journey. Your life is intricately and perfectly designed and written by the Holy Author. It's a series of divine, God-authored plotlines, each designed to shape you more into the image of Christ. Sometimes you are in the spotlight of your own Hero's Journey; other times, you're a supporting character in someone else's story. Either way, the same Author holds the pen. And whether you are in a valley, facing a battle, or standing in the sunlight of victory, God is at work weaving each scene into His greater narrative of redemption and transformation.

Putting It Into Practice

Write: Journal about the current "chapter" of your life. Where do you see God's fingerprints? What trials are testing your faith right now, and how might they be producing perseverance? Is there a past "chapter" you can now see differently because of God's redemptive work?

Think back to and reflect on a past season of your life that now seems like a closed or completed chapter. Using the description of The Hero's Journey in Chapter 2, study that season of your life and align it with the twelve steps of The Hero's Journey.

Pray: Ask God to give you both humility *and* trust – humility to play your role in His story without demanding center stage, and trust to let Him finish the work He's begun in you, no matter how long the journey takes. Repent of taking control, and renew your submission to the Potter's hands.

Act: Choose a worship song (or songs) this week that focuses on God's sovereignty and sing it daily as a reminder that He is writing the story. Spend time *daily* in worship and prayer!

Speak encouragement! Affirm someone else's journey by pointing out where you see God's hand in their life. Encourage them to trust in the Lord's ways and not to give up. Give them this book, and recommend studying it together. In the same way, this week, intentionally serve or bless someone, remembering that you are part of *their* story too.

Release control Name one area you've been trying to "write yourself" and surrender it to God in prayer. Write that area of confession on a piece of paper (or as a background on your phone), and remind yourself daily to surrender, submit, and trust the Lord in that area of your life.

Prayer for the Journey

Lord, You are the Author of my life and the perfecter of my faith. Thank You for *every* chapter — the ones that brought me joy, and the ones that brought me to my knees. Throughout this journey, I have learned that I am not alone in this life. You are always with me, and Your ways are higher and better than my own. Help me to see beyond my own plotline and to trust that You are weaving a far greater story for Your glory. Teach me to lean on You in the wilderness! Show me how to rejoice in Your presence, even in the midst of the battles! Lead me to walk in step with You in every trial and every victory. Write Your truth deep in my heart and give me the courage to live it out. I choose You, Jesus. From this day forward. In Jesus' name, Amen.

Afterword

As I wrote these pages, I found myself walking again through seasons of both pain and praise. What I discovered afresh was this: God doesn't just redeem our stories — He rewrites them with purpose. Even as I was crafting this book, the Lord asked me to revisit painful memories. "Have you fully surrendered this to Me?" and "Do you trust Me in this?" were questions that repeatedly arose in my heart. I found myself again and again having to surrender my pain and scars to Him *and* having to forgive those who have wounded me (Remember Job?).

If you desire to take this journey to the next level and deepen your understanding of this topic, I have also created an in-depth study guide to accompany this book, chapter by chapter. The study guide is filled with thought-provoking questions, prompts, Scripture, prayers, and daily challenges to walk out what you've learned. This study guide is a valuable resource for growing in your understanding of God as the Author of your story. You can find the study guide at ChelseaFain.com/books or by scanning the QR code at the back of the book.

I pray you have had the same God-work done in your heart. I'd love to hear your journey, your trials, your triumphs, and how God has shaped and formed you through your storms. If this book has spoken to your heart, I'd love to hear from you. You can connect with me at chelseafain.com or through social media. Your stories inspire me to keep writing, teaching, and trusting the Author of life Himself.

With love,

Chelsea

APPENDIX I:
Job's Hero's Journey

1. The Ordinary World

Job is living well—wealthy, respected, pious, with a large family and social prestige. Life is comfortable, and he's blissfully unaware of the heavenly conversation between the Creator and the Evil One and the trials that are about to turn his world upside down.

2. Call to Action

Without Job's knowledge, Satan challenges God, claiming Job's faith *in* God is contingent on the blessings he received *from* God. God allows the test, setting in motion the calamities to come.

3. Refusal of the Call

Although Job responds to the initial tragedies with worship, when the turmoil turns on his own body, Job grows silent. He withdraws into pain and wordless agony—refusing to acknowledge the suffering he is wrapped in.

4. Meeting the Mentor

When the agony of his situation swells within Job and begins to cripple his forward movement, his three friends—Eliphaz, Bildad, and Zophar—arrive. Although they act with good intentions, they instead offer misguided, even hurtful, interpretations of Job's suffering.

5. Crossing the First Threshold

The beginning of The Hero's Journey is usually physical, emotional, or spiritual. For Job, it is all three! Job begins to question God's justice and his own understanding of God, marking a significant departure from his previous, unquestioning faith.

6. Tests, Allies, Enemies

Now facing an entirely new world and circumstances, Job must navigate various challenges filled with unanswered questions. Throughout this part of the journey, the hero will encounter allies/friends and enemies, and begin to face various trials and battles. Job loses wealth, children, health, and social standing. Friends—including his own wife!—who started as allies become accusers/enemies. Job wrestles both with them *and* with his own inner turmoil.

7. Approach to the Inmost Cave

This forces Job to come face-to-face with his biggest question and deepest despair. Job approaches a point of deep despair and profound questioning. He longs for an audience with God, seeking answers and understanding.

8. Ordeal

This is the biggest test yet! Job must draw upon everything he has walked through thus far and come face to face with the Creator God in a powerful, personal exchange. As this section almost always involves a metaphorical (symbolic) form of *death* for the hero, Job also experiences a spiritual death concerning his old theology and perception of the Lord. As he encounters the Lord, he challenges God's actions and desires an explanation. This is a pivotal moment of truth-seeking, self-discovery, and profound theological growth for Job.

Job emerges from this Ordeal reborn as a new version of himself, with an entirely new view of himself, his world, and his God. His fear and his pains—although still present—have been broken and bridled. Job's old theology dies, replaced with a deeper understanding of God's power and sovereignty.

9. Reward

This is given to the hero as he walks *through* his Ordeal. The greatest gift is not restored wealth or status, but seeing God and having a personal encounter with Him. This is the ultimate reward to any trial humanity can face: seeing God. At this, Job humbles himself, recognizing his limited perspective and God's infinite wisdom.

10. The Road Back

God restores Job's fortunes and family, but recovery takes years. This restoration wouldn't have been an "overnight" thing, as his family would've taken many years to regrow and be restored. During that time, Job continues to grow in wisdom and in intimacy with God.

11. Resurrection

As he begins the road back to the "new normal," Job experiences a spiritual resurrection of renewed faith. He is no longer defined by his suffering but by his enduring relationship with God. He recognizes that the outcome of his journey will result in far more than just his own change; it will also affect the lives of those around him. We see this specifically in the lives of his new ten children, who are described as being beautiful beyond any others in the land (Job 42:15).

12. Return with the Elixir

Job returns to life with more than just blessings—he carries unshakable maturity, spiritual insight, and a living testimony of God's faithfulness through suffering. We can see the three key elements that usually accompany a hero's return clearly in the ending of Job's story: ***change, success, and proof of the journey.*** Job returns to his community, not just restored in his material possessions but also transformed in his understanding of God and his own faith. He becomes a testament to God's faithfulness and the power of enduring through trials.

APPENDIX 2:
Abraham's Hero's Journey

1. The Ordinary World

Abram begins in Ur of the Chaldeans—a prosperous, polytheistic city—living under his father's household. Childless, he carries a quiet sorrow.

2. The Call to Adventure

God calls Abram to leave his country, his people, and his father's household for a land He will show him (Genesis 12:1). Along with the call comes a promise: Abram will become a great nation, be blessed, and bless all nations—a foreshadowing of the Messiah.

3. Refusal of the Call

While Abram doesn't verbally refuse God's call, his journey is not without hesitation or imperfect obedience. For example, instead of entirely leaving his family behind, he brings along Lot (his nephew), which later causes conflict. And when famine strikes Canaan, Abram flees to Egypt, where he lies about his relationship with Sarah – an act that shows a struggle with fear

4. Meeting the Mentor

God Himself is Abraham's mentor, guiding him through his journey. Through repeated covenant encounters, visions, and even appearances in physical form (as in Genesis 18), God guides, reassures, and strengthens Abraham's faith. Melchizedek, the priest-king of Salem who blesses Abram in Genesis 14, also briefly serves as a mentor figure.

5. Crossing the Threshold

Abram truly crosses into the unknown when he leaves Haran and enters Canaan. This is the beginning of a life of wandering and faith—living in tents, trusting in promises not yet fulfilled, and navigating foreign lands and dangerous kings.

6. Tests, Allies, and Enemies

Abraham's journey is filled with trials: rescuing Lot from enemy kings, enduring famine, fathering Ishmael through Hagar, sending Hagar and Ishmael away at Sarah's insistence, and lying to Pharaoh *and* King Abimalech about his wife. Just to name a few! He struggles with the twenty-five-year delay of God's promises. Despite these tests, Abraham is supported by allies like Sarah, his servant Eliezer, Melchizedek, the Lord Himself, the angels who visit him, and, eventually, his son Isaac.

7. Approach to the Inmost Cave

The deepest inner challenge is waiting for decades to have a child. A year before Isaac's birth, God renews the promise. This year tests Abraham's faith — "Lord, is this *really* happening?" —until the moment he hears his son's first cries.

8. The Ordeal

The climactic test comes when God asks Abraham to sacrifice the promise: Isaac. This command directly threatens the promise Abraham had waited decades for. However, those decades of waiting and trust have prepared him for this moment. Abraham's willingness to sacrifice Isaac (Genesis 22) shows his complete surrender and trust in God. It's the ultimate test of his faith, and demonstrates the tremendous work that God has done in the heart of Abraham — from fearing the Pharaoh and Abimalech over Sarah to now being willing to lay his son's life on the line. Abraham obeys, believing God could raise Isaac from the dead (Hebrews 11:19).

At the last moment, God provides a ram, affirming Abraham's complete surrender.

9. Reward

As a result of his faith and obedience, God renews His promise: Abraham's descendants will be as numerous as the stars, and through them, all nations will be blessed. His reward is not just land or a son, but becoming the spiritual father of *generations*.

10. The Road Back

Though there's no "return home" in the traditional sense, Abraham begins preparing the next generation. He purchases land to bury Sarah, symbolizing his first claim in the promised land, and arranges a marriage for Isaac. These actions show Abraham transitioning from adventurer to founding patriarch.

11. Resurrection

Abraham experiences a spiritual rebirth. He is no longer the man who feared kings because of Sarah, but one who trusts God completely, willing to lay the most precious life on the altar for the Lord.

12. Return with the Elixir

Abraham's "elixir" is the covenant that flows through Isaac, Jacob, the nation of Israel, and ultimately Jesus Christ. Abraham doesn't just benefit himself; his journey becomes a blessing to all nations, precisely as God had promised.

APPENDIX 3:
Joseph's Hero's Journey

1. Ordinary World

Joseph lives in Canaan with his father, Jacob, his mother, Rachel, and eleven brothers. Favored above all, he wears the special multicolored coat his father gave him and is spared manual labor. His brothers' bitter jealousy grows.

2. Call to Adventure

Joseph has two prophetic dreams that depict him at the center of his family, while his brothers and parents bow down to him. He tells his brothers about dreams, which angers them even more.

3. Refusal of the Call

When Joseph is sent to check on them in the fields, the brothers seize the opportunity to act on their resentment. There's no literal refusal from Joseph, but *the brothers reject his* call by throwing him into a pit and selling him into slavery.

4. Meeting the Mentor

Joseph's guiding mentor is God Himself. God's favor and wisdom remain with him—in Potiphar's house, in prison, and in Pharaoh's palace.

5. Crossing the Threshold

Joseph's journey into the unknown world begins when he is forcibly sold into slavery and is taken far from his home, status, and family to Egypt, a dangerous, unfamiliar world.

6. Tests, Allies, and Enemies

His initial time of slavery was only the beginning of his tests. In Potiphar's house, Joseph excels but is falsely accused by Potiphar's wife and thrown into prison. There, the warden becomes an ally, entrusting him with leadership. Joseph interprets the dreams of Pharaoh's cupbearer and baker, predicting the cupbearer's restoration and the baker's execution. Though he asks to be remembered, the cupbearer forgets, leaving Joseph in prison for two more years. Through betrayal, slavery, and prison, Joseph grows in faith, humility, wisdom, and resilience.

7. Approach to the Inmost Cave

When Pharaoh has troubling dreams that no one can interpret, the cupbearer finally remembers Joseph. Summoned from prison, Joseph faces a high-stakes challenge of interpreting dreams that could either change his destiny or return him to obscurity or death.

8. Ordeal

Joseph interpreted Pharaoh's dreams as a divine warning of famine. This moment, filled with risk if he were to misinterpret the dream, became a turning point in his journey. Pharaoh believed him and elevated Joseph to second-in-command over all Egypt, marking the first step in fulfilling his prophetic dreams from decades before.

9. Reward

The reward for his journey to this point was the new position, which came with tremendous power and authority. But, for Joseph, freedom for the first time in *several* years was the sweetest of rewards. With his new position, he began to store grain during the years of abundance, preparing Egypt for the coming famine.

10. The Road Back

The famine drove Joseph's brothers to Egypt to buy food. The "Road back" was really a road of his past coming to *him*. When they arrived, Joseph came face-to-face with the memories of his old life. They do not recognize him, but Joseph acknowledges them. Joseph had the opportunity to exact revenge! However, he chose to test them rather than retaliate. He probes their integrity and transformation through a series of somewhat strange trials.

11. Resurrection

When they returned with Benjamin, Judah offered himself in Benjamin's place—showing the change Joseph hoped to see. Overcome with emotions, Joseph revealed his identity and forgave them. When the brothers returned to Jacob (now called Israel) and he heard about Joseph, he said, *"I'm convinced! My son Joseph is still alive. I will go and see him before I die"* (Genesis 45:28). Joseph lived through a literal resurrection within his family—in their minds and in his relationships with them. This is the emotional climax: a resurrection of family bonds and Joseph's complete personal transformation from arrogant victim to humble redeemer

12. Return with the Elixir

Joseph moves his family to Egypt, ensuring their survival. His wisdom saves not only Egypt but also the future nation of Israel. His personal journey becomes a blessing for generations.

APPENDIX 4:
Moses' Hero's Journey

1. Ordinary World

Moses was born a slave in Egypt during a time of brutal oppression. In an attempt to quell the growing Hebrew population, Pharaoh had decreed that all Hebrew boys be killed. Though marked for death, his mother made a desperate attempt to save him by hiding him in a basket on the Nile River. He was saved by the Princess herself and raised in Pharaoh's palace. He lived between two worlds: Egyptian royalty and Hebrew blood.

2. Call to Adventure

At about 40 years old, Moses saw an Egyptian beating a Hebrew slave. Seeing this take place, something arose within Him to intervene on behalf of the Hebrew slave. I believe this emotional response within him was the call of God in his life. He intervened and killed the Egyptian in defense of the Hebrew slave.

3. Refusal of the Call

The next day, he discovered that his murder was known to many people. He was terrified of the repercussions and fled Egypt to Midian, where he became a shepherd.

4. Meeting with the Mentor

After 40 years in the wilderness, hiding as a shepherd, God had seen significant work done in Moses' heart. God appeared to Moses in a powerful display of His divine power in the burning bush. This moment was both a fresh "Call to Adventure" and a wrestling match of the "Refusal of the Call." Moses resisted, argued with God, and doubted his worth and ability to speak: *"Who am I that I should go to Pharaoh?"* Beginning with this meeting, God Himself becomes Moses' mentor, equipping him for the task.

5. Crossing the Threshold

Moses crossed the threshold when he returned to Egypt, confronted Pharaoh, and demanded freedom for the Israelites. This was his bold first step into the unknown—from shepherd to prophet, from exiled to deliverer, from fearful fleer to influential leader.

6. Tests, Allies, and Enemies

For Moses, this section of his story is the longest. He faced Pharaoh's hardened heart, ten plagues from God, rejection by his own people, and constant rebellion from Israel! Yet God used Moses to display His power: the ten plagues, the Passover, the release of the people, and the parting of the Red Sea. Finally, Moses led the newly freed people into the wilderness and into greater testing.

At this time, he also gained important allies: Aaron, Miriam, and, later, Joshua. His tests continued during his time as leader of the people of Israel. Moses entered his spiritual high point on Mt. Sinai when he entered deep communion with God and received the Law, even as the people fell into idolatry with the golden calf at the foot of the mountain. This repeated itself for Moses: the people's rebellion and complaints, followed by Moses' interceding for the people before God. This cycle of rebellion, judgment, and intercession tested Moses' patience and faith again and again.

7. Approach to the Inmost Cave

The Israelites reached the edge of the Promised Land, marking the most significant test in their journey thus far. Moses sent out twelve spies to scout the land of Canaan. This was a step of faith, meant to inform and encourage the people about their Promised Land, as they stood at the threshold of destiny and fulfillment.

8. Ordeal

Meant to be a moment of celebration and victory for Moses, ten of the twelve spies return instead with a fearful report, saying the land was full of giants and unconquerable cities. Despite the miraculous things Moses witnessed and performed for the people, the people panicked and rebelled instead, weeping and demanding to return to Egypt. Despite Joshua and Caleb's courageous report, the nation refuses to trust God. In this moment of profound betrayal, God declares that this generation would not enter the Promised Land. Moses' greatest heartbreak was to lead them back into the desert for 40 years, watching hope wither in disbelief. He did everything right, but the people refused to follow.

9. Reward

Though devastated, Moses did not abandon his calling. He continued leading faithfully, teaching, judging, interceding, and guiding the new generation. He received further revelation from God, including laws, worship structures, and patterns of justice. His leadership matured during these secondary 40 years of wilderness wanderings, during which he grew into spiritual fatherhood, forming not just a people but a nation ready to walk with God. *This* became his greatest reward.

10. The Road Back

As the wilderness years ended, Moses prepared the people with the book of Deuteronomy. This book stood as a renewal of the covenant, the giving of wisdom, and the appointment of Joshua as his successor. In choosing and appointing Joshua, Moses symbolically passes the mantle of leadership and demonstrates the road moving forward into the Israelites' new "normal."

11. Resurrection

From a hesitant, fearful fugitive to the humble, bold leader, Moses ended his life transformed, full of spiritual insight and courage. He became a completely reborn version of himself. Though he struck the rock in frustration (Numbers 20) and was barred from entering the land, he accepted God's justice with peace and submission. Unlike at the burning bush, he now trusted God, blessing Israel and encouraging Joshua as his final acts.

12. Return with the Elixir

From Mount Nebo, God let Moses glimpse the Promised Land. Though he would not enter it, his mission was complete. He brought God's people to the brink of their destiny. His legacy is not just about land or law, but also about covenant, leadership, and intimacy with God, as he was one of the *few men to encounter the living God* on such a deep, personal, and powerful level. Moses died in God's presence, a powerful gift in itself and a passage into the ultimate "new normal" for Moses into the eternal presence with God. His story became the standard for prophetic and faithful leadership spanning millennia and generations.

APPENDIX 5:
Joshua's Hero's Journey

1. Ordinary World
Joshua began as a Hebrew slave in Egypt. After the Exodus, he became Moses' assistant. Forced to spend 40 years in the wilderness because of the faithlessness of the other ten spies, Joshua lived among the Israelites in the wilderness as a military leader (Exodus 17) and one of the faithful spies (Numbers 13–14). We see him closely connected with Moses, and he even encountered God's presence personally on several encounters, because of his faithfulness to God and to Moses. His life is shaped by obedience, preparation, and quiet faithfulness.

2. Call to Adventure
After Moses' death, God directly commissioned Joshua to lead the people of Israel into Canaan. The call is bold: *"Be strong and courageous... you will lead these people to inherit the land I promised"* (Joshua 1:6).

3. Refusal of the Call

There's no explicit refusal, but Joshua's commissioning includes repeated encouragement from God to "not be afraid," which hints at inner fear or doubt.

4. Meeting with the Mentor

Moses mentored Joshua for decades. After Moses' death, God Himself became Joshua's guide, even appearing as the "commander of the Lord's army" (Joshua 5:13–15).

5. Crossing the Threshold

Joshua led the Israelites across the Jordan River, which miraculously stopped flowing, mirroring the parting of the Red Sea. This marked Joshua's literal and symbolic first significant step from servant into leader, crossing into promise and responsibility.

6. Tests, Allies, and Enemies

Joshua faced an immediate test upon entering the Promised Land: he must confront Jericho, a walled city. Instead of a siege, God commanded a strange strategy: marching silently for six days. Joshua was obedient, and God's power brought down Jericho's walls. As they progressed into the Promised Land, He also dealt with many other tests and trials: failure at Ai due to Achan's secret sin (Joshua 7), the deception of the Gibeonites (who pretended to be allies, Joshua 9), and numerous military conquests, like the battle against the five kings (Joshua 10). He had to discern whom to trust, sought after God's guidance, and united the tribes of Israel in numerous battles. These events taught Joshua always to seek God's guidance *first*. Allies included Caleb, the priests, and faithful warriors from each tribe.

7. Approach to the Inmost Cave

After defeating the southern and northern kings, much of the Promised Land was subdued (Joshua 10–11). However, full possession and unity remained incomplete. The "inmost cave" is not a physical location, but the beginning of the transition to governance and spiritual leadership.

8. The Ordeal

Joshua's most significant test was dividing the land among the tribes (Joshua 13–21), which was a spiritual, political, and emotional test. *The chal-*

lenge was no longer external conquest, but internal peace, unity, and justice amongst the people. Joshua needed to shift from warrior to steward. This ordeal includes:

- Settling tribal disputes.
- Dealing with the hesitation of some tribes to possess their inheritance fully.
- Ensuring faithfulness to God's commands about cities of refuge, Levitical towns, and altars.
- Navigating tensions between the eastern and western tribes (Joshua 22).

9. Reward

Joshua succeeded in allotting the land, and Israel had rest from war (Joshua 11:23). His reward was no longer military victory, but authority, wisdom, and covenant guardianship.

10. The Road Back

Near life's end, Joshua gathered Israel's leaders (Joshua 23–24). He reminded Israel of God's laws and called them to commit themselves fully to God. He warns them of the danger of compromise with foreign nations and gods. Joshua knew that, without continued obedience, their victory would mean nothing. *The road back is not a physical, geographic road. Rather, it's spiritual: a return to covenantal clarity.*

11. Resurrection

Joshua's legacy culminated in his final challenge: *"Choose this day whom you will serve… but as for me and my house, we will serve the Lord"* (Joshua 24:15). He experienced symbolic resurrection. He rose as a patriarchal figure, transformed from soldier to spiritual leader.

12. Return with the Elixir

Joshua dies at 110, having led Israel into their inheritance, rest, unity, and faithfulness. The people continue to serve the Lord throughout his lifetime. *The elixir Joshua brings back is a land of promise, a legacy of obedience, and a covenant identity that shapes Israel's memory and mission.*

APPENDIX 6:
David's Hero's Journey

1. The Ordinary World

David began as the youngest son of Jesse, a shepherd in Bethlehem (1 Samuel 16:11). His world was quiet and obscure—tending sheep, writing psalms, and playing music—far removed from Israel's political turmoil.

2. The Call to Adventure

David's simple life is abruptly interrupted when the prophet Samuel comes to his house. David's standing as the youngest son and his position as shepherd were so overlooked that he wasn't even summoned when Samuel called for all of Jesse's sons. When the Lord rejected Jesse's six older sons, David was summoned and chosen by Samuel. He anointed David as the future king of Israel (1 Samuel 16:13) - which was an act of treason against King Saul. Though the Spirit of the Lord came upon him, David had to wait and suffer before receiving the crown. *(Remember the secret ingredient?)*

3. Refusal of the Call

There's no literal refusal from David, but people in his life seriously reject the call. After being anointed, he returned to the pasture and later served Saul as a musician and armor-bearer. His life outwardly remained the same, delaying the visible fulfillment of his call.

4. Meeting the Mentor

God is David's ultimate guide, but Samuel, and sometimes Jonathan, offer guidance and wisdom along the way. David's early relationship with God, marked by worship and reflection, lays the foundation for his courage and trust. David's psalms are evidence of this inner mentorship through communion with God.

5. Crossing the Threshold

David crossed into the new world when he challenged and defeated Goliath (1 Samuel 17). This act propelled him into national fame and favor, military leadership, and Saul's household. It also made him a threat in the king's eyes. At this threshold, David leaves anonymity behind and enters a world of politics, warfare, and jealousy.

6. Tests, Allies, and Enemies

David endured numerous trials and tests, such as navigating Saul's growing hatred, avoiding assassination attempts, navigating the confusion of mutiny from his followers, and choosing mercy over revenge (cutting Saul's robe, sparing his life), and more! However, those tests are more clearly defined here:

1. The Test of Sudden Fame and Favor (1 Samuel 17–18).
   - After defeating Goliath, David was catapulted into national hero status. He was celebrated with songs (*"Saul has slain his thousands, and David his tens of thousands" 1 Samuel 18:7*), placed in a high military rank, and welcomed into Saul's royal court. Despite this flood of fame, he remained humble and respectful to Saul. He did not let popularity cloud his sense of calling, anointing, or identity.

2. The Test of Envy and Hostility from Saul (1 Samuel 18–19)
   - As David's fame grew rapidly, Saul became jealous of David and tried to kill him multiple times. Yet, David remained in Saul's

service, playing music to calm him even as Saul grew more unstable. Amid the turmoil, David refused to retaliate or speak publicly against Saul. He continued to honor Saul's position as "the Lord's anointed."

3. The Test of Isolation and Exile (1 Samuel 20–23)
- After fleeing Saul in fear for his life, David became an outcast and lived on the run, hiding in the wilderness. He was forced to leave his wife, Michal, and best friend and ally, Jonathan.

4. The Test of Leadership Under Pressure (1 Samuel 22–24)
- During his time in the wilderness, David became the leader of a band of 400–600 disaffected men, many of whom were bitter, in debt, or fugitives. He was thrust into a leadership position of great difficulty to lead and protect these men while constantly avoiding Saul's armies.

In the many trials, *he had to remain faithful, wise, and innocent—even as he was hunted unjustly.* It is estimated that David had to wait approximately *fifteen years* from the moment he was anointed king of Israel until he was actually able to become king of Judah —but he has not yet fulfilled his ultimate promise to become king of all Israel.

7. Approach to the Inmost Cave

David's journey took a dark and morally complicated turn when, exhausted from years of running, he sought refuge among Israel's sworn enemies: the Philistines. He became a vassal of King Achish in Gath and lived in Ziklag of Philistia. Though he outwardly aligned with the Philistines, David secretly raided Israel's enemies to stay in God's favor. This dual life reveals David's deep, internal tension between survival and faith. The "inmost cave" was not just physical exile for David. It was a place of spiritual compromise. This was the deepest phase of isolation, moral tension, and identity crisis. However, God intervened on David's behalf by turning the four other kings of the Philistines against him, giving him a way out of the position of compromise he found himself in.

8. The Ordeal

David's greatest personal crisis came at Ziklag when the Amalekites raided, burned the city, and captured his men's families. His own followers, broken and angry, spoke of mutiny and stoning David. At this moment of utter despair, David turned to his foundation: he *"strengthened himself in the* L{\small ORD} *his God"* (1 Samuel 30:6). Instead of collapsing, he sought divine guidance, rallied his men, and recovered everything that had been taken.

This was the true spiritual climax of his journey: a battle not against armies, but despair. The Ordeal tested David's soul, not his sword, and marked the beginning of his resurrection as a leader grounded in God's strength. This was his personal best victory, a resurrection of faith and leadership before he ever received a crown.

9. Reward

Following his triumph at Ziklag and the death of Saul in battle, David finally steps into a measure of kingship - a reward for the wilderness season he had just walked through. However, He did not rush to claim power but chose to seek God's will *first*. Upon his return to Judah, he was anointed king over the tribe of Judah and began to rule from Hebron. Though the full promise had not yet come to pass, David finally held legitimate authority and led with patience and wisdom, which was developed through the wilderness waiting. He waited in hope and faith for God to bring about the unification of the kingdom at God's perfect timing, refusing to grasp at power prematurely or to take advantage of Saul's fallen house. He reigned over Judah for seven and a half years before moving further into the purposes of God.

10. The Road Back

David's path to full kingship was slow and complex. Saul's son Ish-Bosheth ruled the northern tribes, but David grew steadily stronger without resorting to violence. When Ish-Bosheth was assassinated by his own men, David condemned the act. *He refused shortcuts to God's plan, trusting that God, not human violence, would establish him.*

11. Resurrection

David's resurrection came when all Israel anointed him king. This was not merely a political appointment; it was the fulfillment of the promise made to him by God in his youth. David took Jerusalem and made it the center of both political authority and spiritual worship, bringing the ark of the covenant into the city. This moment symbolized the rebirth of David's calling, no longer as a fugitive or tribal leader, but as the shepherd-king of all Israel, refined by suffering and elevated by God's hand.

12. Return with the Elixir

David's reign brought unity, justice, and the centrality of worship in Israel. God made an everlasting covenant with him, promising his line would endure forever. The "elixir" David brought is a kingdom shaped by divine favor, righteous leadership, and messianic hope—one that ultimately points forward to Jesus, the true Son of David.

APPENDIX 7:
Paul's Hero's Journey

1. Ordinary World

Saul ("Paul" in Greek) began as a devout Pharisee from Tarsus, well educated from youth, and respected among the religious elite. His life was orderly, respectable, and in alignment with Jewish law. From the casual onlooker, he was doing "all the right things."

2. Call to Adventure

Jesus Himself interrupts Saul as he was traveling to Damascus to arrest any followers of "The Way." Along the road, Saul had a blinding encounter with the Messiah and was invited into a radically new mission: to serve the Jesus he had opposed.

3. Refusal of the Call

Unlike his companions, who heard the voice but saw no light, Saul alone was struck blind. For three days, he was spiritually disoriented and confused. He fasted as he wrestled with the collapse of his old identity and theology, unsure of what would come next.

4. Meeting the Mentor

While Saul struggled with the reality of his encounter with Jesus, God sent a Godly man named Ananias to heal, baptize, and mentor Saul. Saul also receives the Holy Spirit at that time, symbolizing divine empowerment for his journey. Ananias serves as a spiritual mentor, and the Holy Spirit also serves as a spiritual mentor throughout the rest of his story.

5. Crossing the Threshold

After his call and time of mentorship, we see in *Acts 9:20* that *"At once he began to preach…"* Saul wasted no time and began preaching that Jesus was the Son of God—a stark contrast to the message he had been carrying on the road to Damascus! Once a persecutor of the way, he stepped into a new world of evangelism for Jesus.

6. Tests, Allies, and Enemies

When Saul stepped away from his cohort of Pharisees—where he was highly respected and climbing the ranks of leadership—he began to face significant opposition from all sides. The Jewish leaders must have been enraged that their leader in quelling the rebellion of "The Way" had a sudden and dramatic conversion to the exact cult he was sent to persecute! He was met with significant (and well-earned) mistrust from Christians and the apostles. And he also faced numerous hardships on his missionary journeys, like stonings, beatings, and imprisonment. When he began his missions to the Greek Gentiles, he began going by the name "Paul," to better cater to his Greek-speaking audience. Along the way, he gains allies like Barnabas, Timothy, Luke, and the other apostles. Paul actually describes his trials and testings in his second letter to the church in Corinth, when he says:

> *"[I have] been in prison more frequently, been flogged more severely, and been exposed to death again and again. Five times I received from the Jews the forty lashes minus one. Three times I was beaten with rods, once I was pelted with stones, three times I was shipwrecked, I spent a night and a day in the open sea, I have been constantly on the move. I have been in danger from rivers, in danger from bandits, in danger from my fellow Jews, in danger from Gentiles; in danger in the city, in danger in the country, in danger at sea; and in danger from false believers. I have labored and toiled and have often gone without sleep; I*

have known hunger and thirst and have often gone without food; I have been cold and naked." (2 Corinthians 11:23-28).

After some time of missionary work and planting churches, Paul returned to Jerusalem, the stronghold of his fiercest enemies. There, he was arrested, beaten, and accused by the religious leaders until he invoked his Roman citizenship and appealed directly to Caesar.

7. Approach to the Inmost Cave

Once he appealed to Caesar, Paul began an even more difficult season of his journey. Paul endured hearings before Felix, Festus, and Agrippa, years of imprisonment, shipwreck, and near-death experiences – all the while staying faithful to his mission. This part of his journey ended with a house arrest in Rome.

8. The Ordeal

The true ordeal was not what most would assume—the chains, shipwreck, or hunger. Paul's ordeal was the climactic confrontation of Paul's mission: to proclaim Christ in the very heart of Rome, before Caesar's court. This was the fulfillment of Jesus' word to him in Acts 9:15: *"He is a chosen instrument of mine to carry my name before the Gentiles and kings and the children of Israel."*

Standing before the empire's most significant authority, Paul's life hung in the balance. Yet he did not waver. The trial was not simply about his fate — it was about the fate of the Gospel reaching the nations. Would Paul shrink back, or would he faithfully bear witness to Christ in the world's most dangerous arena? His Ordeal was total surrender: even if it cost him his life, he would not stop declaring Jesus as Lord.

9. Reward

If anyone made a positive situation out of terrible circumstances, it was Paul. Despite his chains and imprisonment, Paul chose to write letters to encourage and strengthen the churches he had planted. Although we don't see a clear or traditional "reward" for Paul, his reward was greater spiritual influence, clarity of his calling, and an eternal impact that would echo for all time. This is most clearly seen in his letter to the Philippians when he said, *"...I have learned, in whatever situation I am, to be content. I know how to be brought low, and I know how to abound. In any and every circumstance,*

I have learned the secret of facing plenty and hunger, abundance and need. I can do all things through him who strengthens me" (Philippians 4:11-13). This was his prize and his reward: Christ who strengthens him. And that truth continues to resound in the mouths of Christians even today.

10. The Road Back

Instead of returning home, Paul pressed forward with urgency. Knowing his time was short, he poured into building leaders, strengthening churches, and writing letters that would outlive him. His Road Back was not retreat but legacy-building.

11. Resurrection

The end of Paul's story is unknown; however, he likely died a martyr in Rome, but his words and witness lived on. The "resurrection" here is his triumph over fear, persecution, and death through the hope of Christ and a new birth into the Kingdom of Heaven and glorious light.

12. Return with the Elixir – *The Letters of Paul*

Because he died in Rome, this step of his journey would have been carried out posthumously through his letters to the churches. While Paul continues his eternal existence before the Throne of Heaven, the Elixir he brought from his journey was his rich, world-changing writing. These writings became the theological backbone of the church and continue to transform lives worldwide. His journey brought wisdom, transformation, and truth to generations.

APPENDIX 8:

The Hero's Journey of Jesus Christ

1. The Ordinary World

Before His public ministry began, Jesus lived quietly in Nazareth. He worked as a carpenter, honored His parents, and grew *"in wisdom and in stature and in favor with God and man"* (Luke 2:52). Though fully divine, He embraced the ordinariness of human life — the same world He came to redeem. This hidden season reminds us that God values preparation and humility long before public purpose unfolds.

2. The Call to Adventure

Jesus' call was marked by His baptism in the Jordan River. As He rose from the water, the heavens opened and the Father's voice declared, *"This is My beloved Son, with whom I am well pleased"* (Matthew 3:17). This was the divine commissioning — the moment when He publicly stepped into His redemptive mission to reveal the Father's heart and restore humanity.

3. Acceptance of the Call

Unlike every other hero before Him, Jesus did not resist or question His call. Being fully surrendered to the Father, He entered His mission in complete obedience and joy. His willingness to obey even unto death reveals the perfection of His sonship and sets the model for all who would follow Him: *"My food is to do the will of Him who sent Me and to accomplish His work"* (John 4:34).

4. Meeting the Mentor

Throughout His life and ministry, Jesus drew continual strength and direction from His relationship with the Father and the presence of the Holy Spirit. He often withdrew to solitary places to pray (Luke 5:16), demonstrating dependence and intimacy. At His baptism, the Spirit descended upon Him, remaining with Him as His guide and comforter (Luke 4:1). In this, Jesus models perfect reliance, even in divine authority.

5. Crossing the Threshold

After His forty days in the wilderness, where He resisted temptation and affirmed His trust in God's Word, Jesus returned "in the power of the Spirit" (Luke 4:14). He began teaching, healing, and proclaiming, *"The kingdom of God is at hand."* This was the moment He fully entered into the story's conflict: light confronting darkness, truth confronting deception, and heaven invading earth.

6. Tests, Allies, and Enemies

Throughout His ministry, Jesus encountered every element of The Hero's Journey: trials, allies, and opposition.

- **Tests:** Fasting and temptation, rejection in Nazareth, storms, weariness, betrayal, persecution, slandering, and more!

- **Allies:** The twelve disciples, His mother, Mary and Martha, and many others who believed in His name.

- **Enemies:** Religious leaders, demonic forces, and unbelieving crowds. Through each encounter, He revealed divine patience, compassion, and authority, proving that His mission was not to be served, but to serve (Mark 10:45).

7. Approach to the Inmost Cave

As Jesus approached Jerusalem for the final time, the cost of His calling drew near. He entered the city to the sound of "Hosanna," but He wept over it, knowing what lay ahead (Luke 19:41–42). He cleansed the temple, taught His final lessons, and prepared His disciples for the coming sorrow and glory. Every step toward the cross was deliberate: love walking willingly into suffering for the sake of redemption.

8. The Ordeal

The cross was the turning point of all history— the ultimate ordeal! Betrayed, mocked, and condemned, Jesus bore the full weight of human sin, agony, and shame. Even worse, He endured abandonment from the Father. Only Jesus has ever experienced this here on Earth. Yet even in pain, He trusted the Father's plan. His cry, *"It is finished,"* (John 19:30) wasn't one of defeat, but of *completion*. The Hero faced death, and in doing so, broke its power forever.

9. Reward (Victory over Death)

Three days later, the grave could not hold Him. He rose with authority and life, defeating sin and death once and for all. This is the great reward, not only for Himself, but for all of humanity. Through His obedience, we receive forgiveness of sins, restoration to the Father, and eternal hope. The empty tomb is the ultimate declaration that God's story always ends in resurrection.

10. The Road Back

After His resurrection, Jesus appeared to His followers. He built them up, restored their faith, and revealed how all Scripture pointed to Him (Luke 24:27). He reminded them of their purpose: to continue His work through the power of the Holy Spirit. The road back was not a retreat, but a redirection: a return to the world He came to save, now carrying the message and hope of victory.

11. The Resurrection (Transformation)

This stage in The Hero's Journey symbolizes ultimate transformation. In Jesus, it becomes reality. He rose, glorified and eternal, yet still bearing the scars of love. Through His resurrection, humanity itself is transformed: those who were dead in sin are raised to new life in Him: *"If anyone is in Christ, he is a new creation"* (2 Corinthians 5:17).

12. Return with the Elixir

At His ascension, Jesus returned to the Father. However, He did not leave us empty-handed. He brought the victory of redemption with Him to Heaven, but He left us with the promised gift of the Holy Spirit. The "elixir" He gives is salvation, the Holy Spirit, His Word, and the indwelling power of God. Through His commission, *"Go therefore and make disciples of all nations…"* (Matthew 28:19–20), the Hero's story continues in us. We are now part of His ongoing plotline. We have become the living chapters of His glory on earth.

APPENDIX 9

My Story Map

Use the following graphic to reflect on past or current seasons of your life in the lens of The Hero's Journey. How has God been crafting and shaping your story using this plotline?.

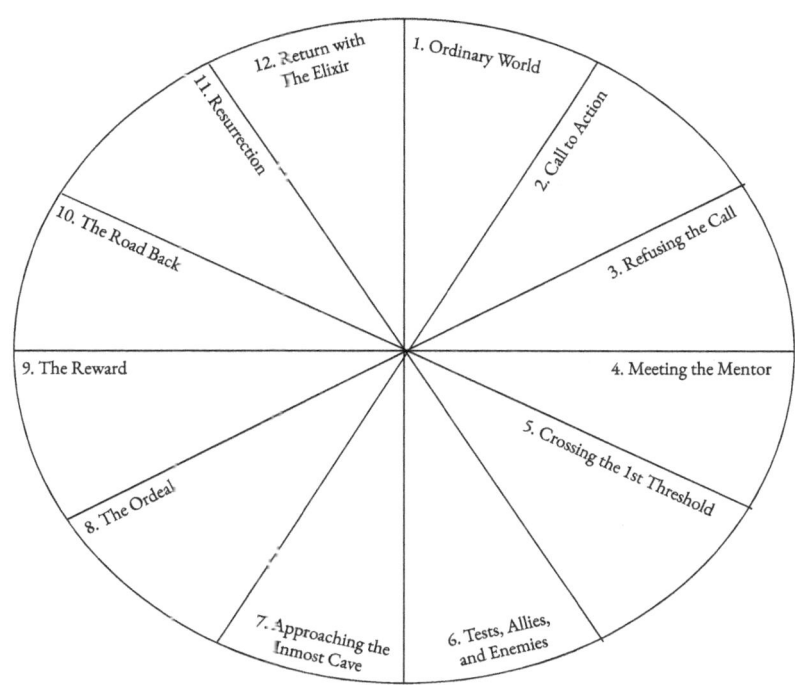

References

Bates, M. "Theology In Research And Practice." *Journal of Psychology and Christianity*, vol. 39, no. 3, 2020, pp. 245-251.

The Bible, English Standard Version. BibleGateway.com.

    Blue Letter Bible. (n.d.). https://www.blueletterbible.org/

Campbell, Joseph. *The Hero with a Thousand Faces*. Joseph Campbell Foundation, 2020.

"Meaning of Numbers: The Number 12." *Bible Study*, www.biblestudy.org/bibleref/meaning-of-numbers-in-bible/12.html. Accessed 25 June 2025.

Pathan, Ravish. "The Lion King : The Hero's Journey." *Unobjective*, 26 May 2019, unobjective.home.blog/2019/05/26/the-lion-king/.

Sorge, Bob. *Pain, Perplexity and Promotion: A Prophetic Interpretation of The Book of Job*. Oasis House, 1999.

Sorge, Bob. *The Fire of Delayed Answers*. Oasis House, 1996.

About the Authors

Chelsea Fain is an author, educator, and worship leader with a Master's degree in Education and a background as a high school English teacher specializing in research and curriculum development. She now combines her academic training with her ministry as a praise choir director, worship leader, vocal coach, and Biblical curriculum writer to help build up her local church. Her passion is to encourage fellow believers to see God's hand in every season. Chelsea and her husband, Joshua, are raising four children, from newborn to teenager, while she homeschools and embraces the beauty and challenges of ministry and motherhood.

Pastor Jennifer Neuschwander is the co-founding pastor of *Life Bible Church* in Harrisburg, Oregon, where she and her husband, Brad, have served since 2001. A lifelong worshiper and gifted prophetic minister, Jennifer's story is one of surrender, resilience, and the redeeming power of God's presence. Through her journey of healing and faith, she has learned to see every trial as part of the divine story God is writing in her life. Today, she continues to minister locally and internationally, leading others into deeper intimacy with the Holy Spirit.

Connect with Me!

You can connect with Chelsea at chelseafain.com, email her at chelsea@chelseafain.com, or on Instagram @ChelseaFainWrites.

Use the QR code to visit ChelseaFain.com

★ Reviews are GOLD for Authors! ★

If this book encouraged you, would you leave a review on Amazon or Goodreads? Your words help this message reach more readers who need hope in their own stories.

Join my mailing list for devotionals, writing updates, new releases, and resources at chelseafain.com/newsletter-sign-up/ or with this QR code:

Thank you for reading *The Divine Plotline*. Be sure to check out these other works by Chelsea Fain at ChelseaFain.com/books or by finding them on Amazon.

The Divine Plotline 31-Day Devotional

The Divine Plotline Study Guide

www.ingramcontent.com/pod-product-compliance
Lightning Source LLC
Chambersburg PA
CBHW020926090426
42736CB00010B/1054